Lean Kaizen

Also available from ASQ Quality Press:

Business Performance through Lean Six Sigma: Linking the Knowledge Worker, the Twelve Pillars, and Baldrige
James T. Schutta

5S for Service Organizations and Offices: A Lean Look at Improvements
Debashis Sarkar

Office Kaizen: Transforming Office Operations into a Strategic Competitive Advantage
William Lareau

Enterprise Process Mapping: Integrating Systems for Compliance and Business Excellence
Charles G. Cobb

Value-Driven Channel Strategy: Extending the Lean Approach
R. Eric Reidenbach and Reginald W. Goeke

Lean Enterprise: A Synergistic Approach to Minimizing Waste
William A. Levinson and Raymond A. Rerick

Lean Strategies for Product Development: Achieving Breakthrough Performance in Bringing Products to Market
Clifford Fiore

The Certified Manager of Quality/Organizational Excellence Handbook, Third Edition
Russell T. Westcott, editor

The Executive Guide to Improvement and Change
G. Dennis Beecroft, Grace L. Duffy, John W. Moran

To request a complimentary catalog of ASQ Quality Press publications, call 800-248-1946, or visit our Web site at http://qualitypress.asq.org.

Lean Kaizen

A Simplified Approach
to Process Improvements

George Alukal and Anthony Manos

ASQ Quality Press
Milwaukee, Wisconsin

American Society for Quality, Quality Press, Milwaukee 53203
© 2006 by ASQ
All rights reserved. Published 2006
Printed in the United States of America
12 11 10 09 08 07 06   5 4 3 2 1

Library of Congress Cataloging-in-Publication Data

Alukal, George, 1945–
  Lean kaizen : a simplified approach to process improvements / George
Alukal and Anthony Manos.
    p. cm.
  Includes bibliographical references and index.
  ISBN-13: 978-0-87389-689-4 (soft cover : alk. paper)
  ISBN-10: 0-87389-689-0 (soft cover : alk. paper)
  1. Reengineering (Management) 2. Waste minimization. 3. Organizational
effectiveness. 4. Industrial efficiency. I. Manos, Anthony, 1963– . II. Title.

  HD58.87.A48 2006
  658.5'15—dc22   2006008817

ISBN-13: 978-0-87389-689-4
ISBN-10: 0-87389-689-0

Publisher: William A. Tony
Acquisitions Editor: Annemieke Hytinen
Project Editor: Paul O'Mara
Production Administrator: Randall Benson

ASQ Mission: The American Society for Quality advances individual, organizational,
and community excellence worldwide through learning, quality improvement, and
knowledge exchange.

Attention Bookstores, Wholesalers, Schools, and Corporations: ASQ Quality Press
books, videotapes, audiotapes, and software are available at quantity discounts with
bulk purchases for business, educational, or instructional use. For information,
please contact ASQ Quality Press at 800-248-1946, or write to ASQ Quality Press,
P.O. Box 3005, Milwaukee, WI 53201-3005.

To place orders or to request a free copy of the ASQ Quality Press Publications
Catalog, including ASQ membership information, call 800-248-1946. Visit our
Web site at www.asq.org or http://qualitypress.asq.org.

Printed in the United States of America

 Printed on acid-free paper

Quality Press
600 N. Plankinton Avenue
Milwaukee, Wisconsin 53203
Call toll free 800-248-1946
Fax 414-272-1734
www.asq.org
http://qualitypress.asq.org
http://standardsgroup.asq.org

To
Elizabeth ("Lizy") Alukal
Thomas Manos, Jr.

Table of Contents

Figures and Tables. . . . .   *ix*
Preface. . . . .   *xiii*
Acknowledgments . . . .   *xvii*

Chapter 1   Introduction to Lean and Kaizen **1**
  What Is Lean?.   1
  Brief History of Lean   2
  Why the Emphasis on Lean Now?   2
  The Wastes of Lean   3
  The Building Blocks of Lean   6
  How to Start the Lean Journey.   8
  Core Concepts of Lean.   9
  Lean Enterprise   10
  What Is Kaizen?.   10

Chapter 2   Change Management and Kaizen Teams. **13**
  The Role of Change Management in the Lean
    Transformation.   13
  Kaizen Teams.   15

Chapter 3   Brainstorming Techniques in Kaizen Events. **17**
  Creativity Before Capital   17
  What Is Brainstorming?   17

Chapter 4   Lean Kaizen in the 21st Century. **21**
  Toyota's Emphasis on Problem Solving and Incremental
    and Breakthrough Improvements   21
  Toyota Uses Basic Quality Tools   22
  Current Lean Kaizen Strategy   25

Chapter 5   How to Perform a Kaizen Event **27**
  The Kaizen Event Eight-Week Cycle   28

Chapter 6   Kaizen Event Examples **45**
5S Workplace Organization and Standardization 46
Accounting—Credits 53
Cell Design 59
Layout 70
Request for Quote to Order Entry 76
Quick Changeover 80
Shipping, Delivery, and Logistics 88
Standard Work in Customer Service 91
A Total Productive Maintenance Event 99
Value Stream Mapping—from RFQ to Delivery 106
Visual Workplace 109

Chapter 7   Cost–Benefit Analysis for Kaizen Projects **125**

Conclusion **131**

Appendix A   Kaizen Event Workbook Example **133**

Appendix B   5S Kaizen Event Workbook Example **145**

Glossary *161*
Bibliography *169*
Index *171*

CD-ROM

Team charter form (page 33) .... TeamCharter.pdf
Project closeout form (page 43) .... ProjectCloseout.pdf
Layout interview form (page 74) .... LayoutInterview.pdf
Time observation form (page 93) .... TimeObservation.pdf
Breakdown analysis worksheet (page 101) ...... BreakdownAnalysis.pdf
Process observation form (page 137) .... ProcessObservation.pdf
Changeover summary chart (page 140) .... ChangeoverSummary.pdf
Appendix A .... AppendixA.pdf
Appendix B .... AppendixB.pdf

Figures and Tables

Figure 1.1   Building blocks of lean. 5

Table 1.1   Variation and waste. 6

Table 2.1   How to sustain lean. 15

Table 4.1   Five whys example. 23

Figure 4.1   Fishbone diagram. 23

Figure 5.1   Kaizen event eight-week cycle Gantt chart example. 28

Figure 5.2   A sample team charter form.. 33

Figure 5.3   An example of a poster promoting a kaizen event................... 34

Figure 5.4   Effort and impact matrix... 38

Figure 5.5   An example of a 30-day action item list. 39

Figure 5.6   Example one-point lesson on how to send a fax. 41

Figure 5.7   A sample project closeout form.. 43

Figure 6.1   Log-in table one-page summary... 49

Figure 6.2   One-point lesson for determining on-hold codes..................... 50

Figure 6.3   Before and after photos of communication board. 51

Figure 6.4   Before and after photos of cabinets.. 51

Figure 6.5   Before and after photos of work tables. 52

Figure 6.6   Credits VSM. 54

Figure 6.7   Backlog of credits... 55

Figure 6.8   An example of an office layout. 57

Table 6.1   Kaizen event goals... 58

Table 6.2   Kaizen event metrics. 59

Figure 6.9   Spaghetti diagram—cell. 62

Table 6.3   Takt time example. 66

Figure 6.10   Standard work combination sheet... 67

Figure 6.11   Load balancing chart... 68

Figure 6.12   Layouts. 69

Figure 6.13   Spaghetti diagram of central processing area........................ 72

Figure 6.14   Excessive paperwork. 73

Figure 6.15   Example of a layout interview form. 74

Figure 6.16   A standardized workstation. 75

Figure 6.17   A layout of the work area before applying lean is on
the left and after is on the right.. 76

Table 6.4   A sample cellular/flow pre-event checklist. 77

Figure 6.18   RFQ flowchart.. 80

Table 6.5   Wastes and lean building block solutions. 81

Figure 6.19   Example of a changeover observation chart. 83

Figure 6.20   Example of a 30-day action item list for QCO..................... 85

Figure 6.21   Photos of the workbench area before the kaizen event
on the left and after on the right.. 86

Table 6.6   Results of the kaizen QCO..................................... 87

Figure 6.22   Standard work process flow diagram. 92

Figure 6.23   Time observation form. 93

Figure 6.24   Standard work combination sheet—before........................... 95

Table 6.7   Reasons for resistance to standard work............................... 96

Figure 6.25   Standard work combination sheet—after............................. 98

Figure 6.26   Breakdown analysis worksheet. 101

Figure 6.27   One good idea sheet. 104

Figure 6.28   Current state map. 107

Figure 6.29   Future state map. 108

Table 6.8   Before and after times for RFQs.. 109

Figure 6.30   A sample communication center.. 114

Figure 6.31   An example of an access panel. 115

Figure 6.32   An example of unorganized bottles on the left and
translucent, color coded bottles on the right........................... 115

Figure 6.33   In the photo on the left, there are no visual lines on
the floor, while in the photo on the right, the areas are
clearly marked. 116

Figure 6.34   The two photos show the same set of stairs, but safety
stripes have been added to the set on the right. 116

Figure 6.35   The white line on the center gear shows alignment
at a glance... 116

Figure 6.36 The large number on the machine identifies the
workstation. 117

Figure 6.37 The control panel is clearly marked to see from
a distance. 117

Figure 6.38 The acceptable range on the gage is clearly marked. 117

Figure 6.39 Visual indicator of possible safety hazard. 118

Figure 6.40 Lubricating oil visual level indicator. 118

Figure 6.41 Organized and clearly labeled shelves. 119

Figure 6.42 The fax machine is clearly labeled in case the user
needs help. 119

Figure 6.43 Dashed lines on floor show how far gate swings open. 119

Figure 6.44 The lines on the floor show work areas and flow. 120

Table 7.1 SMED cost–benefit example. 127

Table 7.2 Sample 5S benefits worksheet. 128

Preface

Lean has been receiving a lot of attention lately from quality professionals, management, and the press. What started out in manufacturing has now migrated to non–shop floor activities. Business support functions, such as sales, customer service, accounting, human resources, engineering, purchasing, within manufacturing firms, as well as purely service organizations like financial institutions, government, and hospitals are now implementing lean.

Those of us in quality became familiar with lean in different ways. Some of us started implementing kaizens in the late 1980s after getting introduced to them by Masaaki Imai's book. Continuous improvement was very important then (as now), what with the focus on statistical process control and other statistical techniques, reengineering, and the introduction of both the ISO 9000 series and the Malcolm Baldrige National Quality Award. The term "lean" came into vogue a little later, first as lean manufacturing and currently as lean enterprise. For many ASQ members, we believe, a good understanding of lean is useful both at work and also careerwise.

Lean (the term was coined by James Womack's group a few years ago), though based on the Toyota Production System (TPS), uses tried and proven, mostly commonsense tools. Toyota learned from Ford Motor Company, U.S. military practices, good old industrial engineering and operations research techniques, U.S. supermarket delivery and inventory control systems, plus German aircraft manufacturing methods, and refined these as well as added a few Toyota-grown improvements to come up with its successful TPS.

Different aspects of lean are useful everywhere. While TPS as a whole is highly beneficial for Toyota (and other automotive manufacturers), imposing all of the same techniques blindly will not be the answer for others. A manufacturing company needs to ask these questions first: Are we make-to-stock or make-to-order? Do we do mostly fabrication or assembly? Do we create discrete widgets or continuously processed product? How about our customers' expectations (quality, cost, and delivery) and our internal lead times? Are suppliers prepared for lean and just-in-time? Are we—senior management, middle management, and shop floor employees—ready? Is the company culture ready to support the transition from traditional manufacturing to lean?

There is no turning back once you start the lean journey (unless you want to continue the flavor-of-the-month syndrome). Lean tools and techniques are simple and rely on common sense, but implementation and sustaining require discipline, motivation, incentives, good change management, and strong, long-term leadership.

From our experience working with a couple hundred companies, the successful ones have a few things in common: (1) management commitment, (2) a well-thought-out master plan, including plans for cultural change, communication, lean training, standardization at the improved level, and rewards/recognition, and (3) alignment of company goals with individual and/or team goals (including addressing the fear of downsizing due to lean improvements). We can also say categorically that the human side of the lean transformation is most critical: the various technical lean tools can easily be taught, but changing the culture, team building, sustainable motivation, alignment of goals, and potential resistance from middle management and unions are issues that need to be carefully considered before embarking on the lean journey.

These days, more and more firms are combining lean with their other improvement efforts. Even the largest corporations are implementing lean, Six Sigma (with emphasis on statistical techniques), theory of constraints, and even total quality management (Baldrige criteria, for instance) and/ or ISO 9001 and its derivatives such as TS 16949, AS9100, and so on, all as a suite of useful tools and techniques. More and more, lean champions, Six Sigma Black Belts, or ISO 9001/TS 16949 management representatives are becoming one function, all using the appropriate tool the correct way, either singly or blended, for problem solving and continuous improvement. The best combination of plan–do–check–act (PDCA) and define–measure–analyze–improve–control (DMAIC) is used wherever possible. As an example, lean experts pull out the appropriate statistical or graphical techniques whenever they encounter the waste ("muda" in TPS terminology) of defects or correction. Lean addresses velocity (time or speed) while Six Sigma looks for stability in the process. Lean tools focus on waste reduction, and Six Sigma methods are used to attack variation. Lean is appropriate for cost and time reduction (directly benefiting throughput and productivity), whereas Six Sigma is good for maintaining/improving quality.

While using lean for transforming our companies, it is important that all employees have training in at least its basic concepts. For Six Sigma implementation, usually only a core group needs to be formally trained. It cannot be overemphasized that in the lean environment, it is essential to focus on *all* employees' contributions through their creativity, problem-solving skills, knowledge of the process, and team brainstorming. "Do not check your brains at the door," "It is not just management who has all the answers," and "Think! Think! Think!" are some of the sayings that have flowed down from Taiichi Ohno, the father of TPS.

Some of the core concepts of lean are: (1) creativity before capital (tapping into the experience, innovation, and knowledge of people working in the process before spending capital on improvements), (2) an improvement that is not so perfect done today is better than the perfect solution that is late (there is always room and the need for further continuous improvements), and (3) inventory is not an asset but a cost (or waste). Lean emphasizes the power of teamwork and consensus through brainstorming.

Where does one begin a lean journey? Value stream mapping is a good starting point, in most instances. The future state map will self-identify the "biggest bang for the buck" improvements, which are carried out as process kaizens.

ABOUT THIS BOOK

The history of how this book came about is as follows: ASQ had contracted the authors to develop a two-day course in lean enterprise and an additional one-day course just on kaizen. These two hands-on courses are being delivered throughout North America, usually four times a year. Based on the success of these programs, ASQ was interested in a practical book on lean kaizen, not necessarily just to complement the courses, but also as a stand-alone offering. Here it is.

All the examples of kaizens presented in the book are from our experiences with real-world lean transformations, which the reader should find useful. After introducing the concepts of lean and kaizen, various building blocks of a lean enterprise are described, so that after completing the book, any reader should gain a foundation of what we understand today as lean or TPS. Chapter 6 describes in substantial detail how to perform kaizens both on the manufacturing shop floor and in support functions or in purely service environments. Another useful feature of the book is Chapter 7, which takes one of the kaizen projects from Chapter 6 (quick changeover using single minute exchange of dies, the so-called SMED technique) and in general terms shows how to perform a cost–benefit analysis on a typical kaizen project.

The intended audience for this book is quality or operational professionals who want to start their lean journey at work or to enhance their career opportunities. The authors recommend that you read this fairly slim volume from cover to cover and then use the various examples as and when needed. The forms, figures, and checklists included in this book and on the accompanying CD-ROM could be customized and used in the readers' own lean journeys when they perform kaizens. The authors will appreciate any comments or suggestions for improvement: authors@asq.org.

Acknowledgments

The authors would like to thank all the people who have impacted their lives on their own lean journeys; this includes all the people that they have worked with, taught, coached, and learned from. As a special mention, for examples in this book and other assistance, the authors would like to extend a debt of gratitude to:

Nick Adler, Vice President of Operations, Fort Dearborn Company, Niles, Illinois

Demetria Giannisis, CEO/President, Chicago Manufacturing Center, Chicago, Illinois

Mark Sattler, Director, ProMedica Laboratories, Toledo, Ohio

Pat Thompson, General Manager, Modern Drop Forge, Blue Island, Illinois

1

Introduction to Lean and Kaizen

WHAT IS LEAN?

In the last ten years or so, a new term has entered our vocabulary: "lean." Executives and decision makers, especially in senior management, quality, operations, engineering, and human resources have been hearing of lean in a context other than dieting. What is it?

Lean is a manufacturing or management philosophy that shortens the lead time between a customer order and the shipment of the parts or services ordered through the elimination of all forms of waste. Lean helps firms in the reduction of costs, cycle times, and non-value-added activities, thus resulting in a more competitive, agile, and market-responsive company.

There are many definitions of lean. Here is one that is used by the Manufacturing Extension Partnership of National Institute of Standards and Technology, a part of the U.S. Department of Commerce: "A systematic approach in identifying and eliminating waste (non-value-added activities) through continuous improvement by flowing the product at the pull of the customer in pursuit of perfection." Lean focuses on value-added expenditure of resources from the customers' viewpoint. Another way of putting it would be to give the customers:

- What they want

- When they want it

- Where they want it

- At a competitive price

- In the quantities and varieties they want, but always of expected quality

A planned, systematic implementation of lean leads to improved quality, better cash flow, increased sales, greater productivity and throughput, improved morale, and higher profits. Once started, lean is a never-ending journey of ever-improving processes, services, and products. Many of the concepts in total quality management and team-based continuous improvement are also common to the implementation of lean strategies.

BRIEF HISTORY OF LEAN

Most of the lean concepts are not new. Many of them were being practiced at Ford Motor Company during the 1920s or are familiar to most industrial engineers.

A few years after World War II, Eiji Toyoda of Japan's Toyota Motor Company visited the American car manufacturers to learn from them and to transplant U.S. automobile production practices to the Toyota plants. With the eventual assistance of Taiichi Ohno and Shigeo Shingo, the Toyota Motor Company introduced and continuously refined a system of manufacturing whose goal was the reduction or elimination of non-value-added tasks (activities for which the customer was not willing to pay). The concepts and techniques that go into this system are now known as Toyota Production System (TPS), and were recently reintroduced and popularized by James Womack's group in the United States under the umbrella of lean manufacturing.

Lean concepts are applicable beyond the shop floor. Companies have realized great benefit by implementing lean techniques in the office functions of manufacturing firms, as well as in purely service firms such as banks, hospitals, and restaurants. Lean manufacturing in this context is known as *lean enterprise*.

WHY THE EMPHASIS ON LEAN NOW?

Lean is especially important today as a winning strategy. Some key reasons are:

1. To compete effectively in today's global economy

2. Customer pressure for price reductions

3. Fast-paced technological changes

4. Continued focus by the marketplace on quality, cost, and on-time delivery

5. Quality standards such as TS 16949:2002 and ISO 9001:2000

6. Original equipment manufacturers (OEM) holding on to their core competencies and outsourcing the rest

7. Higher and higher expectations from customers

8. The need for standardized processes so as to consistently get expected results

To compete successfully in today's economy we need to be at least as good as any of our global competitors, if not better. This goes not only for quality, but also for costs and cycle times (lead time, processing time, delivery time, setup time, response time, and so on). Lean emphasizes teamwork, continuous training and learning, production to demand (pull), mass customization and batch-size reduction, cellular flow, quick changeover, total productive maintenance, and so on. Not surprisingly, lean implementation utilizes continuous improvement approaches that are both incremental and breakthrough.

THE WASTES OF LEAN

Waste of resources has direct impact on our costs, quality, and delivery. See Sidebar 1.1. Conversely, the elimination of wastes results in higher customer satisfaction, profitability, throughput, and efficiency. Excess inventory, unnecessary movement, untapped human potential, unplanned downtime, and suboptimal changeover time are all symptoms of waste.

Ohno of Toyota compiled what he called the "seven deadly wastes." In the United States, it is felt that a very important waste was omitted from this original list: the waste of not fully utilizing the precious asset of people. So in this book, the authors consider there to be eight wastes (*muda* in Japanese) associated with lean. They are:

1. *Overproduction.* Making more, earlier, or faster than is required by the next process.

2. *Inventory.* Excess materials or more information than is needed.

3. *Defective product or service.* Product requiring inspection, sorting, scrapping, downgrading, replacement, or repair. This also affects information, if it is not accurate and complete.

4. *Overprocessing.* Extra effort that adds no value to the product (or service) from the customer's point of view.

5. *Waiting.* Idle time for staff, materials, machinery, measurement, and information.

Waste

Eliminate waste by identifying and purging all non-value-added activities.

- Waste is any activity that does not add value to the final product or service for the customer.

- Value-adding activity is an activity that transforms or shapes raw material or information to meet customer requirements. It is generally accepted as approximately five percent of total work/time.

- Non-value-adding activity is an activity that takes time, resources, or space, but does not add to the value of the product or service itself. It is approximately 70 percent of total work/time.

- Non-value-adding but necessary activities, for example, accounting and meeting governmental regulations, take approximately 25 percent of work/time.

6. *People.* The waste of not fully using people's abilities (mental, creative, skills, experience, and so on).

7. *Motion.* Any movement of people (or tooling/equipment) that does not add value to the product or service.

8. *Transportation.* Transporting information, parts, or materials around the facility.

Eliminating these eight wastes is the major objective of lean implementation. The continuous reduction and/or elimination of them results in surprisingly high reductions in costs and cycle times. If we do a root cause analysis of each of the eight wastes, we can come up with the appropriate lean tool to tackle the causes identified. See Figure 1.1. The various lean tools and techniques, called lean building blocks, are described later in this chapter. If, for instance, long lead times and missed delivery dates are major bottlenecks, identifying the underlying reasons might lead to a focus on setup times, machine downtime, absenteeism, missed supplier shipments, quality problems, and overproduction resulting in excess inventory. The lean improvement could be implemented as a kaizen event.

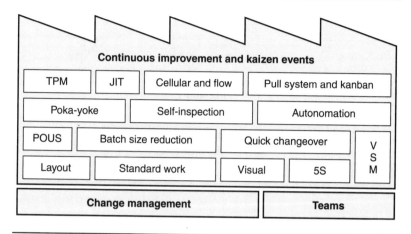

Figure 1.1 Building blocks of lean.

Let's look at one example in detail: the primary reason for overproduction and carrying excess inventory might be due to long process changeover times, in which case the correct tool (or lean building block) to use will most likely be single minute exchange of dies (SMED) or quick changeover techniques. This SMED project will be done as a kaizen.

Changeover time is defined as the time between the last good piece off the current run and the first good piece off the next run. The traditional changeover assumption is that long runs are necessary to offset the cost of lengthy changeovers. This is not valid if the changeover time can be reduced as far as possible (less than 10 minutes if the SMED technique is applicable) and standardized at that level so that we are confident that a good piece from the next run can be made in a certain time period. The changeover improvement process typically includes the following steps:

- Identify and form the changeover improvement team (operators, manufacturing/quality engineers, setup specialists, material handlers, tool/jig/fixture makers, maintenance technicians, supervisors/team leaders, and so on).

- Document the current changeover (videotape where possible).

- Through brainstorming, analyze the changeover and identify ways to reduce, eliminate, consolidate, or mistake-proof steps and convert from internal to external time/tasks. *Internal time* is when the machine is stopped, whereas *external time* is when the machine is producing the previous part.

- Implement improvements and monitor results.

Table 1.1 Variation and waste.

• Poor layout	• Not following procedures
• Long setup time	• Instructions/information not clear
• Poor workplace organization	• Poor planning
• Poor equipment maintenance	• Supplier quality problems
• Inadequate training	• Inaccurate gauges
• Use of improper methods	• Poor work environment (for example, light, heat, humidity, cleanliness, clutter, and so on)
• Statistically incapable processes	

- Streamline all aspects of setup operations.

- Standardize the improved changeover.

Besides attacking overproduction/inventory wastes, quick changeover can result in the reduction of lead time, defective product, and space requirements while improving productivity, flexibility, and producing smaller batches with more variety (mass customization).

Many of the wastes could be associated with variations in processes; statistical tools, including the Six Sigma DMAIC methodology, might be appropriate to attack such wastes. Lean and Six Sigma are not mutually exclusive—rather they are complementary. Some firms use the appropriate combination of lean, Six Sigma, theory of constraints, and elements of TQM in their constant drive for continuous improvement and competitive advantage.

Table 1.1 presents sources of waste due to variation and nonstandardization. Each of the items, if currently present in a process, can be analyzed and improved using lean tools in a kaizen mode.

THE BUILDING BLOCKS OF LEAN

The tools and techniques used to introduce, sustain, and improve the lean system are sometimes referred to as the lean building blocks. Many of these building blocks are interconnected and can be implemented in tandem. For example, 5S (workplace organization and standardization), visual controls, point-of-use storage (POUS), standard work, streamlined layout, working in teams, and autonomous maintenance (part of total productive maintenance) can all be constituents of introducing a planned implementation effort. The building blocks include:

- *5S.* A system for workplace organization and standardization. The five steps that go into this technique all start with the letter *S* in Japanese (*seiri, seiton, seison, seiketsu,* and *shitsuke*). These five terms are loosely translated as sort, set in order, shine, standardize, and sustain.

- *Visual controls.* The placement in plain view of all needed information, tooling, parts, production activities, and indicators so everyone involved can understand the status of the system at a glance.

- *Streamlined layout.* A layout designed according to optimum operational sequence.

- *Standard work.* Consistent performance of a task, according to prescribed methods, without waste and focused on human movement (ergonomics).

- *Batch-size reduction.* The best batch size is one-piece flow, or make one and move one! If one-piece flow is not appropriate, reduce the batch to the smallest size possible.

- *Teams.* In the lean environment, the emphasis is on working in teams, whether it be process improvement teams or daily work teams.

- *Quality at the source.* This is inspection and process control by employees so they are certain that the product or information that is passed on to the next process is of acceptable quality.

- *Point-of-use storage.* Raw materials, parts, information, tooling, work standards, supplies, procedures, and so on, are stored where needed.

- *Quick changeover.* The ability to change tooling and fixtures rapidly (usually in minutes) so multiple products in smaller batches can be run on the same equipment.

- *Pull/kanban.* A system of cascading production and delivery instructions from downstream to upstream activities in which the upstream supplier does not produce until the downstream customer signals a need (using a kanban system).

- *Cellular/flow.* Physically linking and arranging manual and machine process steps into the most efficient combination to maximize value-added content while minimizing waste. The aim is single-piece flow.

- *Total productive maintenance (TPM).* A lean equipment
  maintenance strategy for maximizing overall equipment
  effectiveness.

Besides these building blocks, there are other concepts or techniques that
are equally important in lean: value stream mapping (VSM), just-in-time
(JIT) methods, error-proofing (poka-yoke), autonomation (jidoka), change
management, root cause analysis and problem solving, and policy deployment (hoshin planning).

Since lean is a never-ending journey, there is always room for continuously improving.

HOW TO START THE LEAN JOURNEY

Lean will not work if it is viewed as merely a project, as single-point solutions,
or as a vehicle for downsizing. It works best if deployed as a never-ending
philosophy of improvement. Many firms have appointed and empowered
lean champions for successfully implementing their lean transformations;
these champions help others as mentors, trainers, group facilitators and
communicators, and act as the drivers of continuous improvements, plan-
ners, evaluators, and cheerleaders celebrating each success. They also help
in permanently capturing the gains by standardizing at the higher levels of
performance as lean is implemented, so as not to slip back.

The starting point of lean initiatives could be any one or more of the
following:

1. Value stream mapping. A value stream map (VSM) studies the set
   of specific actions required to bring a product family from raw
   material to finished goods per customer demand, concentrating
   on information management and physical transformation tasks.
   The outputs of a VSM are a current state map, a future state map,
   and an implementation plan to get from the current to the future
   state. Using a VSM, we can drastically reduce the lead time
   closer and closer to the actual value-added processing time by
   attacking the identified bottlenecks and constraints. The implementation plan (typically of short duration, such as 12 months)
   acts as the guide for doing so. Bottlenecks addressed could be
   long setup times, unreliable equipment, unacceptable first-pass
   yield, high work-in-process (WIP) inventories, and so on.

2. Lean baseline assessment. Uses interviews, informal flowcharting,
   process observations, and analysis of reliable data to generate an

as-is situational report from which would flow the lean improvement plan based on the identified gaps.

3. Provide training in lean to a critical mass of employees in teach–do cycles. Lean implementation should continue immediately after the training.

4. Implement the basic building blocks first, for example, 5S, visual controls, streamlined layout, POUS, and standard work. Then build on with the higher-level tools and techniques, finally achieving flow production based on customer pull.

5. Pilot project. Choose a bottleneck, constraint, or new product area to do breakthrough lean improvement (use the kaizen event approach). Then, with the lessons learned, migrate lean implementation to other areas.

6. Change management. Align the company's strategies and employees' goals, then change the culture from the traditional push production to lean pull. This should eventually result in a philosophical change in people's daily work life.

7. Analyze the internal overall equipment effectiveness (OEE) and the OEE losses. A Pareto chart of these losses will identify the biggest bang for the buck to indicate where to start the lean journey.

CORE CONCEPTS OF LEAN

Here are some important concepts that will be useful to keep in mind while preparing for the lean transformation:

- Creativity before capital. In lean, instead of spending large sums of money on capital expenditures, team brainstorming of ideas and solutions is emphasized. People working in the process are brought together to tap into their experiences, skills, and brainpower to generate the plan for reducing wastes and for process improvements.

- A not-so-perfect solution that is implemented today is better than a perfect solution that is late. Just do it *now*!

- Inventory is not an asset, but a cost/waste.

- Use the proven PDCA methodology for deploying improvements—both incremental and breakthrough.

- Once started, lean is a never-ending journey.

- Remember that, typically, 95 percent of lead time is not value-added. Collapsing the lead time closer to the actual processing time by squeezing out non-value-added time and tasks results in both cost and cycle-time reductions. Henry Ford knew this in 1926, when he said, "One of the most noteworthy accomplishments in keeping the price of Ford products low is the gradual shortening of the production cycle. The longer an article is in the process of manufacture and the more it is moved about, the greater is its ultimate cost."

LEAN ENTERPRISE

Enterprisewide lean implementation has slightly different challenges compared to deploying lean in manufacturing. On the shop floor there is a tangible product that is being transformed, so the utility of the tools and techniques described in this chapter for cost and cycle-time reduction in the processing of raw materials into usable finished goods is fairly evident. In the office functions in a manufacturing firm or in a strictly service firm, many of the same tools and techniques are applicable, be it in a slightly modified form. Instead of hardware one looks at value-adding processing and/or use of information (or software). For example, in a hospital lean can be applied to reduce wait times, improve human interactions with patients, have correct supply levels on hand, and better utilize resources. The concept of streamlining and purging of non-value-added steps in the order-to-cash cycle (or RFQ-to-cash cycle) has helped many companies. Bottlenecks are attacked using the PDCA model and the appropriate lean building blocks.

WHAT IS KAIZEN?

Kaizen, a combination of two Japanese words (*kai* + *zen*), literally means "change for the better." This is loosely translated as "continuous improvement" in English. The common use of the term in the United States means breakthrough improvement, implemented as a project or an event. Unlike incremental improvements, breakthrough improvements usually have a beginning and an end.

A few years ago, the term kaizen blitz (meaning substantial improvements in a flash, and service marked by the Association for Manufacturing Excellence) was popular. In Japanese, the term *kaikaku* is more commonly used for what we understand as a kaizen blitz or event. Nowadays people refer to such lean breakthrough improvements more and more as kaizen events or just as kaizens. Kaizens pave our lean journey.

2

Change Management and Kaizen Teams

THE ROLE OF CHANGE MANAGEMENT IN THE LEAN TRANSFORMATION

As managers, we know that we can not stand still in the face of global competition because our rivals are not standing pat, but improving their processes and systems to catch up or overtake us. Also, if we do not improve, sooner or later our customers will prefer them over us. We lose market share, our margins deteriorate, and sales revenue and profitability suffer. So if we know that we need to improve, the question then becomes, Why don't we?

Proper planning and implementation management is the key in obtaining enduring success with lean deployment. Lean is not a quick fix; we are kidding ourselves if we think that lean implementation is easy. Lean concepts are simple, but sustainable deployment is difficult. Success requires not only good change management practices, but also the integration of lean into the overall business strategy. The "flavor of the month" syndrome should be avoided.

Complete implementation of lean might not be for everybody, so a well-thought-out master plan based on cost–benefit analysis is a useful preliminary step. Great benefits from lean implementation are derived by first focusing on understanding our processes (and comparing them to our competitors'), the product families we make, the environment we operate in, the competitive situation we face, and then using the right lean tool at the right time. For example, a firm producing parts to customers' orders rather than to stock will face different challenges, as will a fabrication operation versus an assembler.

Senior management's long-term support and commitment is absolutely essential in implementing lean. Some of the factors in the success of lean implementation are due to senior executives' active role in:

- A planned approach to lean implementation, rather than single-point solutions

- Providing the needed resources

- Appointing lean champions

- Empowering and involving employees, with an emphasis on teamwork and cooperation

- Communicating well, both top-down as well as bottom-up

- Managing expectations, fear of job loss

- Ensuring that everybody understands the need for change, as well as their new roles as change is implemented

- Creating an atmosphere of experimentation in a risk-taking environment, with a safety net for trial and error

- Creating a good reward and recognition program, suggestion system, and gain sharing program

- Making everybody understand the competitive reasons for, and benefits of, lean within the company as well as for themselves personally

- Creating a vision of the future state after the change

- Introducing a performance measurement system based on meeting company goals

- Analyzing and sharing costs versus benefits

- Emphasizing the accountability of everyone

In many cases, implementing pilot projects first in a kaizen mode gets immediate buy-in from skeptics. The success achieved from these quick hits can then be migrated to other areas in a planned approach. Ultimately, lean has to become the daily work habit or operating philosophy of the whole firm to be sustainable.

Starting the lean process is comparatively easy, but sustaining it over the long haul takes robust planning, discipline, commitment, patience, an environment of tolerating some risks or mistakes, a good reward and recognition program, and peoples' receptivity to change and growth. See Table 2.1. Many managers have found that the three essential ingredients for successful lean implementation are: (1) sustained, hands-on, long-term commitment from senior management, (2) training in the lean building

Table 2.1 How to sustain lean.
• Internalize it into daily work
• Remember it is a never-ending process
• Provide discipline, motivation, and incentives
• Continue visible management commitment
• Keep communication channels open
• Standardize so as not to slip back
• Use lean champions
• Job rotation

blocks for all employees, and (3) good cultural change management in the transformation from the traditional push to the lean pull mentality.

We hear again and again that, "Lean is simple, but implementation is not." What this means is: the lean tools and techniques are not rocket science, but the human side of lean is not as easy to manage. The human side of lean includes both change management and teamwork.

KAIZEN TEAMS

There are two types of lean teams: (1) daily work teams that work on incremental improvements and standardization activities all the time, as part of their daily work, and (2) kaizen teams (process improvement teams) that come together for a set purpose and disband after the kaizen event is over. These teams may then join up with other teams (or form new improvement teams) for further kaizen activities.

An example of a lean daily work team is a multiskilled, cross-trained group working in a cell, or a TPM team (consisting of management, engineers, maintenance, and operators), or customer service team. Either these people work together every day, or are responsible for a particular function whenever needed. In other words, they do not disband, unlike the kaizen teams.

Kaizen teams tend to be multiskilled, cross-trained, and cross-functional. Each member receives training in lean, kaizen, and teamwork, including basic consensus-building and conflict resolution, problem-solving techniques, and so on, if they do not already have such training. A good facilitator is essential. The facilitator keeps the kaizen team activities on track, and helps in team formation/building, team rules/guidelines, and consensus/decision making. The facilitator should be experienced in brainstorming and lean techniques.

A kaizen team will typically have up to 10 participants (seven is an ideal number). Team discussions and decisions involve all members and should be based on facts and data to the extent possible. Management should display its commitment to lean by providing sufficient resources (time, space, access to facilities and information, training, and so on) to the team to complete the kaizen satisfactorily without interruptions or distractions. The team members should be freed up to focus on the kaizen at hand, away from the pressures of daily work. Chapter 5 goes into great detail on how to form a team and execute a kaizen event.

3

Brainstorming Techniques in Kaizen Events

CREATIVITY BEFORE CAPITAL

The first motto of lean, and consequently of kaizen, is to utilize the creativity, experience, skills, knowledge, and innovation in people first, before looking for solutions based on capital expense, high technology, expensive machinery, and so on. Tapping into the collective wisdom of the humans working in the process to be improved (as well as outsiders in the kaizen team environment) is a powerful way of arriving at breakthrough improvements. Good facilitators working with the kaizen team efficiently collect ideas, help in brainstorming solutions, and reach consensus quickly. Improvement goals are agreed upon; quantifiable targets are set. These go into the plan of the kaizen PDCA sequence. The plan is then implemented, monitored periodically to check performance against plan, and any necessary midcourse correction is made if found to be necessary. Otherwise the realized improvements are captured through standardization at the higher level.

WHAT IS BRAINSTORMING?

The aim of brainstorming is to collect the creative ideas from all the kaizen team participants without criticism or judgment and to come to consensus decisions. There are two distinctive phases in a brainstorm: the idea generation phase and the discussion/consensus phase.

No discussions are allowed during the idea generation phase, nor are groans, grimaces, or criticism of any kind. The facilitator encourages everyone to freewheel and piggyback on each other's ideas. Since the greater the number of ideas the better, participants are told not to hold back. See Sidebar 3.1. As the quantity increases, typically the quality of ideas also goes up. Either the facilitator or a scribe from the team will capture all ideas and display them for all members to see on a flip chart or a white board.

Brainstorming Warm-Up Example

A method to get the creative juices flowing and to show the team how brainstorming is performed can be done with this quick and easy exercise.

Perform the brainstorming session in a round-robin technique, meaning that you proceed around the room to each person and everyone will offer an idea for improvement. If a person does not have an idea, just have him or her say "pass" and move on to the next person. Before starting, remind everyone that there is no judging other's ideas. The goal during this session is the quantity of ideas, not the quality. Encourage everyone to give even outrageous ideas or to piggyback on others' ideas.

When you are ready to proceed, write on a board or flip chart the topic of this brainstorming session, "How can we improve the lunchroom?" Usually, you will get some laughs because of the subject. Go around the room at least twice, noting how many suggestions are given. Make a special point to praise those who come up with wild ideas or those who add on to other's ideas. When you notice that you get a lot of "pass" answers, this is probably the time to stop and perform a report out. Discuss the number of ideas generated in a short period of time and allow the team to share their comments about the session.

To begin the idea generation phase, the facilitator defines the subject of the kaizen brainstorming session by writing it down for everybody to see and digest. In the round-robin method, the facilitator then goes around one by one asking for ideas one at a time until all ideas are exhausted. Each idea, as it is called out, is written down and displayed for all to see.

In an alternate method, the facilitator will ask the team members to raise their hands to be called on to verbalize the ideas. The second method saves time, but shyer team members might not participate as vigorously. Since everyone has a brain and creativity is the essence of brainstorming, we do not want to leave any ideas unexplored.

A third way is for every team member to write down all their ideas on individual sticky notes and then fix them to the flip chart or white board.

This has the advantage of anonymity (so as not to upset any team member), but piggybacking on each other's ideas will not be possible.

After all ideas are captured, the discussion phase begins. At this time, ideas can be discarded, put on hold, combined, prioritized, and so on. Sometimes alternate solutions will be identified as well. Consensus is continuously built during this phase. *Consensus* is an outcome that all the kaizen team members can support, and none will actively oppose. It is neither a unanimous vote, nor is it a majority vote. Even though everyone might not be totally satisfied with a particular decision, at least all members can live with the outcome. The facilitator understands and communicates to the team that consensus requires sufficient time, active listening and participation by all, skills in seeing others' point of view during any conflict resolution, creative thinking, open-mindedness, and a process orientation (rather than personalities).

There are a few team rules to be followed by the kaizen members. The facilitator conveys these guidelines at the start of the kaizen event. They are:

- Discussions involve all team members.

- Members listen to every suggestion and show respect for each other's ideas.

- Members have a problem-solving attitude rather than finger-pointing or placing blame.

- There should be no silent disagreements; express and discuss all concerns openly.

- Challenge the current way the process is done; there are no sacred cows.

- All team members are equally informed. For example, the team leader's friends on the team are not fed any inside information.

- The team leader (or process owner or the highest stakeholder or an aggressively vocal team member) does not take over the meeting.

- Decisions are based on facts and data, not perceptions, emotions, or personalities.

One advantage of kaizen projects is that as the team brainstorms ideas, if any particular decision needs to be supported by current data, the team can check the fact or information by reviewing the videotape, time study, VSM (or even a process map), or just simply going out to the shop floor, office, or facility where the process is currently occurring. This is quite frequently done to understand the current state better, to explain a point to the outsider(s) on the kaizen team, or to clarify/verify certain assumptions. To facilitate this type of verification, it is important that the kaizen event be carried out in a quiet room close by the process being improved. In a four-day kaizen, it is not unusual for the team as a whole (or a subteam) to go back and forth as many as 10 times during the team activity period, besides during the scheduled breaks, and before and after the kaizen activities each of the four days.

Knowledge of simple root cause analysis and problem-solving tools by the kaizen teams is helpful. So, during the first morning of the lean kaizen event, the facilitator makes sure that all team members are on the same page as far as the understanding of elementary quality and other basic tools (such as the fishbone diagram, Pareto chart, flowcharting, the process model, benchmarking, and five whys) as well as the ground rules for brainstorming. During the discussion of the process model, the concept of supplier–inputs–process–outputs–customer (SIPOC) is explained. If any team members require additional training in these techniques, the eight wastes of lean, or in the building blocks used to attack the various wastes, that should also be provided.

4

Lean Kaizen in the 21st Century

TOYOTA'S EMPHASIS ON PROBLEM SOLVING AND INCREMENTAL AND BREAKTHROUGH IMPROVEMENTS

Lean kaizen, as practiced at Toyota, has helped that automotive firm to become a global giant, be consistently profitable, and increase market share year after year. The TPS (of which lean kaizen is the bedrock) evolved by utilizing practical problem-solving and continuous improvement techniques rigorously. From hard experience Toyota learned early that merely increasing productivity as the only goal does not work.

JIT manufacturing (producing and transferring to the next customer only what is needed when it is needed) directly resulted in less overproduction, inventory, and the other wastes of lean. JIT helped Toyota transform from a traditional push environment based on forecasts and multiple scheduling into a customer demand–based pull system. Lean kaizen efforts created, and further refined, useful tools such as the andon (visual display boards or lights), kanban (information signals to trigger production, replenishment, and conveyance), poka-yoke (error-proofing), and heijunka (to level production batch size and variety). Toyota also placed a laser beam focus on the human side of lean in changing the internal culture to a team-based environment, where people followed proven standards as if by second nature, and where all the lean tools and techniques became an integral part of daily work life. Workers are encouraged to be thinkers and problem solvers instead of mere rote doers. The lean kaizen culture requires employees to use their heads instead of just their hands. This emphasis on creativity and idea generation eventually led to a drastic reduction of the various deadly wastes and cut down on total lead times.

Just reducing the quantity or batch size to decrease the wastes of excess inventory and overproduction, without paying attention to defects, results in not being able to meet customer requirements in quality, cost, or delivery. At Toyota, if a quality problem is detected, the line is immediately stopped and human intervention corrects the situation. Producing what is needed, when needed, mandates building quality into the process. Eventually, through continuous lean kaizens, the concepts of jidoka (autonomation or human-based automation) and quality at the source were incorporated. This required not only using poka-yoke techniques wherever possible, but also empowering workers to be responsible for the quality of their own work. Line workers were trained as inspectors of their output where needed and as problem solvers. They were provided the necessary tools and standards, and process controls such as statistical control charts were emphasized. Various forms of visual controls were generated and implemented with the help of the process owners themselves.

Standard work is the cornerstone for identifying when things go wrong at Toyota. Consistency and uniformity of value-adding work performed the same way by everyone, across shifts, results in high quality and predictability. Focused thinking about what went wrong or about how to improve the process further leads to additional kaizen opportunities. Items that are running smoothly, and per the standard, do not require any further control or extra people to inspect the product or to maintain the line.

TOYOTA USES BASIC QUALITY TOOLS

Toyota believes in simple tools and solutions wherever possible. There is a great focus on rapid root cause analysis and permanent problem solving by the use of the five whys technique. Employees are given practical training so that instead of deduction, they are able to get to the genuine root cause. See Table 4.1 on the five whys method to root out problems and to fix the process for good. Remember, defective processes lead to defective products. The answer to the fifth why reveals that the real root cause is a worn gasket and not the blown fuse, as originally identified.

Besides the root cause analysis tool of five whys, the Ishikawa diagram or the fishbone diagram is also widely used to drill down to the true cause. See Figure 4.1. Other simple and beneficial techniques are the process map, Pareto chart, histograms, run chart, scatter diagram, check sheets, along with different matrices, charts, and graphical tools. Benchmarking is used to set aggressive goals for kaizen projects. Spaghetti diagrams (see Sidebar 4.1) are useful for understanding the non-value-added path taken by operator and product or information in the company. In traditional facilities, the movement of staff, tooling, materials, and information can look like a bowl of spaghetti. Another technique used in lean kaizens is the analysis

Table 4.1   Five whys example.

Question	Answer	Fix
1. Why did the machine stop?	It blew a fuse.	Replace fuse.
2. Why was there an overload?	The bearing lubricant wasn't adequate.	Add more lube.
3. Why was the lube inadequate?	The lube pump wasn't working right.	Replace the pump.
4. Why wasn't the pump working right?	The axle wore out.	Replace the axle.
5. Why was the axle worn out?	Because sludge got in.	Replace the gasket.

Adapted from Taiichi Ohno.

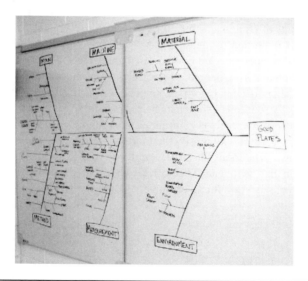

Figure 4.1   Fishbone diagram.

of internal versus external time or steps. An internal task can be done only when a machine is stopped, whereas external steps can be accomplished in parallel with a machine producing value-added work. Other useful lean terms and tools such as VSM, takt time, line balancing, pull system, and continuous flow, are described elsewhere in this book.

Spaghetti Diagram

A spaghetti diagram is a useful tool to show material, people, and information flow within a work area. This will make the wastes of motion (walking) and transportation (moving items about) very apparent. It will also help with uncovering other types of wastes such as waiting or overprocessing. This is an extremely powerful tool when you want to look at waste in a department or for creating a more efficient layout. It is called a spaghetti diagram because it will look like a bowl of spaghetti when you are done because of all the lines drawn on it.

The basic concept is to make a scale drawing or sketch of a work area and trace the path of material, people, or information flow over a specified period of time. A scale drawing of the area works best. If you do not have one, create a sketch of the area with footprints of equipment, furniture, walls, doors, windows, and so on. It is important to measure the distances carefully so that the actual distances traveled can be calculated. Trace a separate line each time material, people, or information are moved in the work area. Using different color pens or pencils or using different types of lines like dashed or solid may help. Track these movements over a period of time, such as 15 minutes to an hour, depending on the amount of travel. Obviously, the more movement, the more lines are drawn. The more lines that are drawn, the more difficult the diagram may be to read. Then calculate the distances covered. See the sample diagram for an example.

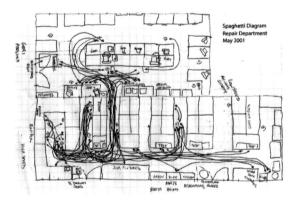

Spaghetti Diagram
Repair Department
May 2001

Kaizens are handled using the PDCA cycle. The approach that the kaizen team comes up with is the *plan,* implementing the plan is the *do,* monitoring performance versus plan is the *check,* and taking midcourse correction if the performance does not meet the plan or standardizing at the improved level if the targets are met would be the *act.* The standardize–do–check–act (SDCA) cycle is relevant for problem-solving efforts. If we find that something is wrong while monitoring (checking) routine work being done to a set standard, we need to solve the problem and bring the process back to the standard. Thus PDCA is used for continuous improvement efforts and SDCA is more closely tied to problem-solving activities. Standardize first using SDCA, and then improve using PDCA.

CURRENT LEAN KAIZEN STRATEGY

Toyota's strategy is to remain profitable and to increase global market share by focusing on lasting cost reductions without compromising quality, features, availability, or customer satisfaction. High quality is the minimum requirement just to play in the extremely competitive international marketplace of the 21st century. As competition has become global, the need for the transfer of the lean techniques to the point of production and point of use has also increased. Lean kaizen training and application, along with institutional knowledge management, has helped Toyota remain a continuously learning and innovating organization.

Suppliers are brought into the fold as well. To be able to produce better goods more cheaply, supplier collaboration and long-term partnering are essential. Lean logistics and lean supply chain play an increasingly important role. Suppliers are taught lean kaizen techniques through the TPS. The value in shifting the suppliers' focus from just the original equipment manufacturer (in this case, Toyota) to the end consumer (the car buyer) is emphasized.

The future belongs to the nimble firm like Toyota that anticipates and understands the needs and wants of the end user and incorporates them into its products. Today, this continuously evolving future requires the organized use of incremental and breakthrough continuous improvement methods through lean kaizens.

5

How to Perform a
Kaizen Event

There are many ways to prepare for and perform a quick, three- to five-day kaizen event. Experience shows that the better you prepare, the better results your event will have. Kaizen events can occur on the spur of the moment. For example, events can occur because we have some extra time, orders are low, or we have extra people. But using your VSM or design teams to plan the events is always best. A design team is a group that creates the plan for lean implementation based on the building blocks of lean (see Figure 1.1, page 5) or based on the requirements of management.

This chapter contains an example of how to get the most out of your lean kaizen events with advance preparation and follow-up. This technique goes beyond just performing the kaizen event itself, it helps give the team the highest probability for a successful kaizen.

Many companies are performing kaizen events (also known as kaizen blitz, quick kaizen) on a regular basis with extremely good results. Other organizations struggle with scheduling events, performing the kaizen, getting people to participate, and then ultimately sustaining the gains originally achieved. When it comes to lean implementation, it is not the tools that are difficult to use, but rather the human side of implementation that can cause troubles. The following methods will help companies chart a clear path for successful execution and implementation of quick improvements. There are other documented methods to perform kaizen events that are extremely effective. If you have another method and it works, then stick with it. If you feel that you are not getting the most out of your projects, then you may want to try this technique or combine it with what you already have. If you haven't performed kaizens before, this method may help you prepare for your first foray into holding these events.

THE KAIZEN EVENT
EIGHT-WEEK CYCLE

Kaizen means change for the better or to break something down into its components for improvement. A kaizen event is a short, focused project that is typically three to five days in length. Companies have even performed one-day mini kaizen events for specific applications. Performing improvements in this mode helps alleviate one of the biggest problems for organizations—not finishing projects that they start. As one manager put it, "We have a lot of takeoffs, but not many landings." Since this is a short, focused method, we are not searching for perfection, but rather we are looking for improvement.

This eight-week cycle allows an organization to adequately prepare for the event, hold the event, and set in place the discipline needed to sustain the new, improved state. Three weeks prior to the actual event, the team meets and prepares for the project. In the fourth week the team actually determines the current state, creates ideas for improvement, and implements the best ideas. This is the kaizen event. The next three weeks are used for follow-up activities, to ensure that the project has a definite end, the gains are sustained, and the results are publicized. See Figure 5.1. Then the event is closed out.

Pre-Event: Planning and People

Pre-event preparation is typically done during the planning phase of the VSM or by the designated design team. This can be up to a year in advance, but will probably be reviewed a week to a month before the kaizen event. Use the VSM or design team plan to determine the type of event and possible target area. Updating the current state VSM or creating a process-level

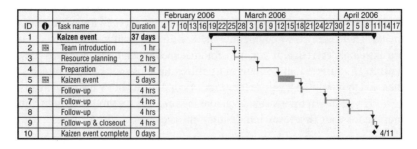

ID	❶	Task name	Duration	February 2006	March 2006	April 2006
1		**Kaizen event**	**37 days**			
2	▦	Team introduction	1 hr			
3		Resource planning	2 hrs			
4		Preparation	1 hr			
5	▦	Kaizen event	5 days			
6		Follow-up	4 hrs			
7		Follow-up	4 hrs			
8		Follow-up	4 hrs			
9		Follow-up & closeout	4 hrs			
10		Kaizen event complete	0 days			4/11

Figure 5.1   Kaizen event eight-week cycle Gantt chart example.

VSM (for an example see Chapter 6, Accounting—Credits) may be help-ful during this stage. The data used in the map may be verified during the event week.

Project Leader

The design team or steering committee will determine the project leader. The project leader is typically the supervisor or manager from the target area. This person is responsible for completing the event. This person has enough pull within the company to get things done and also has some sign-off authority to purchase needed (low-cost) items for the event. Remember, in lean we preach, "Creativity before capital." The project leader will also help support the lean champion and step in as a facilitator if needed.

Lean Champion

Lean champions are subject matter experts in the building blocks of lean. They have extensive knowledge in that area of lean, have led and facilitated projects before. These are your local experts for the kaizen event. The design team may select the champion or the project leader may help select which champion to use for the event. Lean champions will facilitate the event, do the training, help maintain records, and keep the group on schedule.

Team Members

A good size for a kaizen team is about 7 to 10 participants. If you have too many people it becomes like "herding cats." If you have too few people, not as much will get done or one person may try to overpower the group. Team members can be volunteers or assigned. To find volunteers, post a sign-up sheet in the work area, lunchroom, or other high traffic areas.

Have a mix of hourly and salaried employees. Include internal (or exter-nal) customers and suppliers. If the event is on the shop floor, make sure someone from the office is on the team. If the event is in the office, make sure someone from the shop floor is on the team. Have an outsider who can ask the question, "Why?" It is important to have that outsider point of view. The outsider is able to question or see things that others in the process may miss because they have been doing it so long the same way they can't see the forest for the trees anymore. Include someone from the next scheduled kaizen event so that that person has some exposure to a kaizen and can help spread the word about lean.

Here is a list of potential candidates or departments to draw from: accounting, internal/external customers, customer service, design team members, engineers, inventory control, information technology, lean cham-pion, maintenance, area manager, operators, president, project leader, pur-chasing, quality, sales and marketing, scheduling, steering committee members, supervisors, support functions, internal/external suppliers, technicians, value stream manager, and vice presidents. By no means is this list all-inclusive, but it can give you a starting point for selection.

Make sure you have people from the work area on the team and preferably from all shifts. There is nothing worse than having other people come into an area and change things around without enlisting the help of the people who actually work there. Be ready to address the questions, "Why was I picked?" or "Why wasn't I picked?" Obviously the ones that were chosen for this event were selected for a reason, let them know the rationale. Let other people know that everyone will be on a team eventually, so even if they weren't used this time, they will be on a team in the future.

Don't avoid the people that you think may give you the most resistance. Through experience we have found that these people become the greatest advocates of lean because you were able to show them what is possible in a short period of time. Also, you may want to enlist the help of unofficial leaders in your organization. You know who these people are. They might not have any fancy titles, but they are well respected by others.

Make sure that it is understood that the participants have to be present for all the meetings, the entire kaizen event, and for the follow-up actions. If there are reasons why they can't be present, you may want to consider other participants for that event. Also, make sure that their boss knows this too. There may be managers who will say, "I can't give up anybody for that long!" The truth is that they probably can (like a vacation), but they just don't want to. Remind them that there will be events in their area to help improve their processes. So the sooner they have people participating in these events, the sooner those people will understand and hopefully start to implement lean ideas in their area.

Have someone from accounting available (if someone from accounting is not on the kaizen team already) on the morning of the last day to help determine cost savings for the project. Make sure that representatives from management, the design team (if applicable), and associates from the target area are present the afternoon of the last day for a close-out presentation.

Finally, make sure the team members have enough time to plan for their activities to be covered during their absence. Many times it is expected that managers work on the kaizen event during the day and then catch up on any important items in the evening. Also, allow for any travel plans (flights, hotels, rental cars, and so on) if team members are not local.

Week 1

This is when the team formally meets for the first time. As everyone knows, just because you throw a group of people together and declare, "You're a team!" it isn't necessarily so. At this point they are still a group. To become a team takes time, respect for others' abilities, communication, trust, and accomplishment.

This first meeting is meant to be brief, typically 30 minutes to an hour in length. The team will perform introductions, discuss the scope of the project, have a brief overview of the project, list expectations, and determine communication methods. A review of the VSM, if available, may be useful at this point. Create your own pre-event checklists specific to particular types of events (for example, 5S, quick changeover, layout, standard work, cells, TPM) to help make this step more efficient.

Team Introductions

Have all members of the team introduce themselves, including items such as title or position, number of years with the organization, previous experience with lean, and expectations of the event. If they do not have any expectations at this time (since they may not have any opinion or knowledge of the project), they can add them later at the next meeting.

Project

Have the project leader, design team member, or lean champion describe the scope of the project including items such as who, what, when, where, why, and how. The leader can also discuss the goals of the project. Some of the goals will be determined as the team prepares for the event. If it is practical, have the team go to the target area by the end of the meeting so members can get a sense of the scale of the project. The target area is the physical location and boundaries of the event. If it isn't practical to go to the target area, another alternative is to have pictures of the area. Make sure everyone is clear about the extent and scope of the project. We want to reduce or eliminate any assumptions, preconceived notions, or perceived barriers to implementation. Have a brief discussion of what data collection may be required to show before and after improvements. If it is found that the data needed are not already being collected, discuss with the project leader how to start getting the information before the events starts.

Overview

Have a brief (10 to 15 minute) overview of the type of project. For instance, if it is a 5S event, have a presentation that gives the basic concepts of 5S. If it is about quick changeover, have an overview of quick changeover techniques. Since some members of the team may have never heard of lean before or not participated in this type of event, it is important that they hear the fundamentals of what you are trying to accomplish. Some companies use PowerPoint slide presentations, videos, or stories from a person who participated in a previous event.

Another idea is to give each of the team members an article or short book on the subject and have them read it before the next week's meeting. One method is called lunch and learn. Have the team meet over lunch to discuss the book or articles and prepare a list of questions to help aid the discussion. Team members don't need to be experts before the event, but they do need to have a basic idea of what is expected.

Team Charter

It is a good idea to have the team fill out a team charter form like the one in Figure 5.2. This just recaps key items and provides space for additional information related to the next meetings. Make sure the team discusses how it will communicate with other people in the organization including those in the target area. Team members can do this by creating a one-page newsletter, announcements, short stand-up meetings, posters, e-mails, and so on, about the event. See Figure 5.3 for an example of a poster. At this point make sure team members know what their action items are for the next meeting, thank them for attending, and adjourn the first meeting.

Week 2

During this meeting the team does much of the preparation for the event, though the meeting shouldn't take more than two hours. The lean champion will help facilitate this portion of the meeting since that person has experience from previous events and may be a wealth of information regarding materials or supplies needed for this event. Also, if the design team has created a boilerplate list of items, this may prevent the team from trying to reinvent the wheel (like the pre-event checklists mentioned previously). Consider outside resources that may be needed (such as electricians, millwrights, riggers, vendors, and so on) to be better prepared for the event and to help schedule their time.

Items and Materials Needed

Use lessons learned from previous events, previous experience, and brainstorming to determine items or materials needed for the event, including items for the training room (LCD projector, screen, flip charts, markers, sticky notes, room layout, and so on). Create a list and make sure that the project leader gets the items needed. This is extremely useful to do in advance because it gives everyone a chance to think about the project in more detail and it will reduce the waiting time to get the items during the event. For some events, it may take time to order an item and have it shipped

Team Charter

Team name

Participants
    Leader
    Scribe
    Timekeeper

Problem statement

Impact

Resources

Timeline

Results

Figure 5.2   A sample team charter form.

Coming soon to an
area near you . . .
Improvement!

Figure 5.3   An example of a poster promoting a kaizen event.

and delivered. For instance, if you are performing a layout event you may want to include: clipboards, pencils, erasers, rulers, a digital camera, note pads, and a magnetic board with magnets. It is helpful to have specific kits of materials ready for the event, such as cleaning and labeling supplies for 5S. You can even discuss the lunch menu for the week of the actual event as long as it doesn't take longer than five minutes!

Communicate, Communicate, Communicate!

Take time to communicate with others in the target area about the upcoming event, including all shifts. People want to know what's going on in their area. They tend to get nervous if they see a band of people coming into their work area to change things around. Use the items that you determined from the first meeting (announcements, newsletter, posters, and so on). Consider setting up a communication board for the event that says, "Coming soon . . . improvement!" This can be a portable board on which the team can post important information about the event for everyone to see.

During this time offer the others not on the project a chance to give ideas or opinions that would help make the event a success. These can be verbal as long as someone from the team writes them down. This will show the people that you have listened to their ideas and are taking them seriously. If the idea is beyond the scope of the project, write the idea down anyway and tell them that this might be helpful on another project. Do not turn down any ideas. Remember, "no" now doesn't mean "no" forever. This is your chance to start to build buy-in.

Metrics

As a team, determine the metrics that can be captured to show improvement. For example, if the event is related to quick changeover, you may want to record the changeover time, number of internal and external steps, the amount of material waste, walking distance, and so on. Even if the metrics aren't perfect, it will give everyone on the team a chance to think about how to capture the improvements, and monitor and sustain the gains. These metrics have to be meaningful, especially to the people in the target area. They need to be something that they have input to or control over. If you force metrics on them that they have no way of achieving, you are just defeating the purpose of the kaizen event.

Week 3

This meeting should last an hour, at the most. Take time to review items or materials to make sure you have what you need. This still gives adequate time to get many of the needed items in before the event. Also take time to review the metrics. It may be appropriate to change some of the metrics at this time. Discuss any possible obstacles to a successful implementation. This will give the team a chance to have an open and honest discussion about resistance or difficulties it may encounter. Make sure that you spend time to communicate with the target area people again.

Week 4

This is where the rubber hits the road; this is the week of the actual kaizen event. A typical three- to five-day event will have the following elements (expand or contract based on the scope and size of the project):

Day 1

• Introduction of team members and objectives	8–9 AM
• Kaizen event training	9–10 AM
• Break 10 minutes	
• Kaizen team training exercise 1	10:10–11:10 AM
• Kaizen team training exercise 2	11:10 AM–12:00 PM
• Lunch as a team	12–12:30 PM
• Set up walk-through (plant tour, historical data interpretation)	12:30–1:30 PM
• Current state data gathering	1:30–4 PM
• Break 10 minutes	2:30 PM

Days 2 and 3

- Two breaks at 10 AM and 2:30 PM for 10 minutes each
- Lunch at 12 PM for 30 minutes on both days
- Continue current state review
- Calculate time and distances or other measures
- Start brainstorming opportunities for improvement
- Build team consensus and select actual tasks
- Start implementation of ideas

Days 4 and 5

- Two breaks at 10 AM and 2:30 PM for 10 minutes each
- Lunch at 12 PM for 30 minutes on both days
- Continue with improvement implementation
- Document improvements
- Identify action items to address in order to continue kaizen event effort
- Calculate savings
- Presentation to company personnel

Introductions and Training

This is a recap of the team members, project scope, and metrics. Perform some training related to the kaizen event. Make sure you include some kind of in-class, hands-on exercise. For some this may be a review, for others this may be the first time they have heard of lean. Be prepared for all types of participants and adult learners.

Another alternative is to perform train–do cycles. For instance, if you are performing a 5S kaizen, you may want to do some training on "sort" and then go to the target area and perform "sort." Then do some training on "set in order" and then go to the target and "set in order," and so on.

Determine the Current State

We must know how we are doing things today in order to improve them. The goal here is to remove any assumptions or preconceived notions that people have about the process. There are several methods to capture the current state including videotaping the process, flowcharting, conducting interviews, gathering personal observations, creating spaghetti diagrams, or performing time studies. Break down the process step by step so that everyone has a solid understanding of the operation. They don't have to be experts in it; as a matter of fact, it is a good idea to have someone on the team (like an outsider) who will question why things are done in a particular fashion. Review any data collected beforehand and the VSM.

Brainstorm Ideas for the Future State

During this phase, the goal is to get as many ideas as possible for improvement. One method that is effective is to give everyone a stack of sticky notes and a pen. Have the team brainstorm silently for about 15 minutes. Then go around the room and have each person present one idea. If another person has a similar idea, capture that one too. Post these on a nearby wall. After the team has exhausted all its ideas, have the team create an affinity diagram by grouping like items in categories. Have the team give general names to the categories like: training, equipment, procedures, visual controls, and so on. Chapter 3 includes more detail about brainstorming.

Determine Which Ideas to Implement

During this phase, have the team members separate the groupings into three classes: *A* are items that they can do themselves without anyone's permission, based on who is on the team. *B* items are those with which they may need help from another department such as maintenance, information technology, or accounting. *C* items are those where management needs to make the final decision; typically these are items that have a sign-off level higher than anyone on the team. The reason to break the ideas into these classes is to show the team that they have more control over their work area than they think. It is not uncommon for the *A* items to be 60 percent to 70 percent of all the ideas generated.

As a team, cull the items from the list that do not make sense for this project, are out of scope, or would take too long to implement. Next, prioritize the items for implementation. An easy method for this is to determine the effort and impact of the idea. Once again, as a team, determine if the idea has a low, medium, or high effort to implement and if it has a low, medium, or high impact. Work on the items that have low effort and high impact first. See Figure 5.4.

Implement the Ideas

After determining which ideas to implement, have the team divide up the work. Try to have at least two team members work on an item so that people aren't working on their own. Make sure that the team members haven't taken too many tasks or are expected to be in two areas at once. Also,

		Low	Medium	High
	High	No!	Avoid	Maybe
Effort	**Medium**	Avoid	Maybe	Maybe
	Low	Avoid	Maybe	Yes!
		Low	**Medium**	**High**
			Impact	

Figure 5.4   Effort and impact matrix.

have the group determine if it has the right supplies (see week 2). A 30-day action item list is a perfect way to track these items to make sure that the right things are completed—on time! A 30-day action item list would include the item, person responsible, materials needed, other helpers, and a way to track if the item is complete or not. Figure 5.5 shows a sample list. The project leader, facilitator, and lean champion should be checking the status of the progress as they go, but have the team perform a review at lunch and at the end of the day to stay on target.

Closeout and Presentation

Have the team create a short (30 minutes to one hour) presentation for management and people from the target area. This will take some time, so be prepared to give the team about two hours or so to organize and rehearse. Have everyone on the team explain a portion of the kaizen event, but do not force anyone to speak in front of the crowd if he or she is nervous or unwilling. At this point it is also helpful to have someone from accounting help calculate any savings from the kaizen. Remember, management speaks the language of money, so anything that we can do to help improve communications, the better.

A closeout agenda may look something like this:

- Team introduction and project description—include scope and goals (3 minutes)

- Before state—brief description of the current condition (2 minutes)

Project:

Project Name

Status		Classification	Count	Percent
0 = Open	7	A = No assistance needed	4	33.3%
C = Closed	5	B = Other resources needed	2	16.7%
		C = Management help necessary	6	50.0%
Total 12		Total	12	
Complete 42%				

Classification

☐ A = No assistance needed
☐ B = Other resources needed
☐ C = Management help necessary

Percent Complete — 68% / 32%

ID	Status	Classification	Priority	Description	Original completion date	Actual completion date	Assigned to (Primary)	Assigned to (Other)	Effort	Impact	Comments
				Organize							
10	C	A		Label the rack in pressroom			Graham	Pedro	L	H	
11	O	A		Have the plate maker separate bags by copy and color			Phil	John	L	H	
12	C	A		Different color sticky notes for each reason on hold			Graham	Pete, Maria P	L	H	
13	O	A		Mark and label cabinets			Roger	Pedro	L	L	Used colored clips
14	C	B		Have job bags pre-glued			John	Phil	L	L	Cabinets are new, need to decide what goes in
15	O	B		Organize area outside plate room			Phil	Homer	L	L	Small only, can't glue medium or large
16	O	C		Send e-mails when schedule is updated or changed			Roger	Robert	L	H	Cart parking area? Reduce WF damage in transit
17	O	C		Create final floor plan			John	Bob	M	H	
18	C	C		Move plate punches for better access			John	Steve	M	M	See #18
19	O	C		Install basket to catch proofs instead of falling on the floor			George	Ralph	L	L	
20	C	C		Figure out plate storage area with new processing line going in			Chris	Christy	M	M	See #18
21	O	C		Lock schedule after certain time (in the morning)			Roslyn	Lisa	H	H	

Figure 5.5   An example of a 30-day action item list.

- Wastes—show examples of the eight wastes of lean (10 minutes)

- Building blocks of lean—show examples of which building block helped (10 minutes)

- After state—quantitative, qualitative, and financial measures (7 minutes)

- Follow-up and lessons learned—30-day action item list, next steps, and things to avoid next time (2 minutes)

- Support—thank the other people who helped during the project (1 minute)

- Ah-has and question-and-answer time—have each team member share something that made a big impression on them because of this event and open it up for questions and answers (25 minutes)

There will be an official closeout at the end of the eight-week cycle to fully consider the impact made. Make sure you invite the attendees in advance so they have time to work it into their schedules.

Weeks 5, 6, and 7

Follow-Up

There are those lean practitioners who say there should be no follow-up to an event, that everything that could be completed should be completed in the three to five days. There are two main reasons that follow-up is a good idea. First of all, experience shows that even with planning, not everything can be completed in three to five days, like moving equipment or utility lines (electrical, water, air). Consider another example of painting lines on the floor. It may be preferable to use temporary tape to determine if the lines are in the right spot or even the right shape and size. After using the temporary lines for a while, the workers can tell you if there need to be any changes. Also, it may be difficult to paint lines while operations are being performed, so sometimes painting is scheduled on the weekends or off-shifts.

The second and probably more important reason to do follow-up is that it helps build the habits and discipline of lean and reinforces the concepts. It will give the participants time to practice what they have learned in a hands-on manner.

Make sure that managers and supervisors understand up front that members of the team are required to participate in these follow-up activities. This is part of the full commitment to the project. The project leader is required to maintain and update the 30-day action item list. This should be shared and communicated with all the team members, the lean champion, and the people who work in the area.

Training and Communication

At this point there have probably been many changes, and in order to sustain the gains, all people affected by the modifications need to be informed and possibly retrained. This is also time to solicit more input for improvements from other workers in the area. An extremely effective tool to train people in the new methods is to create one-point lessons.

A one-point lesson is a visual tool that can be used to train somebody on how to do one thing in about 10 minutes or less. See Figure 5.6 for a one-point

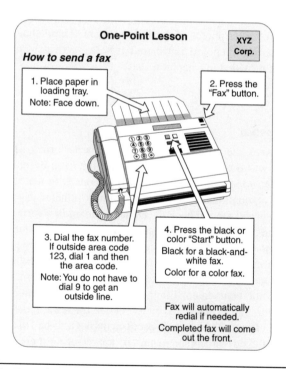

Figure 5.6   Example one-point lesson on how to send a fax.

lesson on how to send a fax). It is not used to train someone on a complex task, but rather to break tasks into smaller, more manageable steps.

Standard work also may be developed to ensure compliance to the new methods. Standard work is specific about the sequence, content, timing, and outcome of a process. Audit the process to make sure that people are following the new methods. It is extremely important to give them immediate feedback if they are not following the new standards. This is vital for creating adherence, consistency, and discipline. Remember, you are striving for reliability and reduction in variation.

Hold brief stand-up meetings at the communication board with two employees at a time. The reason for only two employees is that if you try to do this with the entire department, nobody will be able to see the items on the communication board. Also, with two people, it may be easier to get them to discuss opportunities for improvement. It doesn't have to be the project leader who does this portion solo. Other team members can be recruited to help out so no one is tied up for too long.

Another great communication tool is a one-page summary. On a one-page summary, the team states the problem, solution, and benefits along with before and after photos of the improvement. These should be posted on the communication board and shared as best practices with other areas. Examples are provided in Chapter 6.

Week 8

Project Closeout

During this week the official project closeout is performed. The previous closeout that was done at the end of the actual kaizen event is a striking communication tool. This portion of the closeout is to really capture the total qualitative, quantitative, and financial improvements. Also, the results and lessons learned are fed back to the design team or steering committee to improve the process and to make sure your lean implementation plan is on track. Lessons learned can include: how well the planning portion went, if goals were met, if the resources were adequate and available, and the level of teamwork. See Figure 5.7 for a sample closeout form. At this time your VSM should be updated with the new and improved information.

At this point an official celebration is due for reward and recognition of the team's efforts. This doesn't necessarily need to be financial. Many people are satisfied with other means of appreciating their involvement, contributions, and success. The key is that they are recognized in a public way. It can be something as simple as buying lunch, t-shirts, gift cards, an

Project Closeout Form

ID	Item	Rating				
1 = Very poor　　　2 = Poor　　　3 = Average　　　4 = Good　　　5 = Very good						
Vision		1	2	3	4	5
1	Did the end result meet the original desired results?					
2	Was the original plan realistic?					
3	How do others view the project?					
a	Customers					
b	Team members					
c	Stakeholders					
d	Other					
Plan		1	2	3	4	5
4	Project met budget specifications?					
5	Project met timeline specifications?					
6	Changes were successfully managed?					
7	Adequate resources were identified and utilized?					
Implementation		1	2	3	4	5
8	The plan was implemented successfully?					
9	The plan was revised sufficiently and in a timely manner?					
10	Resources were available?					
11	Review meetings were productive and regularly held?					
12	Project documentation was adequate?					
Close		1	2	3	4	5
13	The project ended in a timely manner?					
14	Project documentation was complete?					
15	All team members participated in project evaluation?					
16	Lessons learned and gaps were documented?					
17	Opportunities for improvements were documented and reviewed?					
Other		1	2	3	4	5

Comments:

Figure 5.7　A sample project closeout form.

article in the company newsletter, or a visit from the president of the company. Since you know your organization best, you'll know what works for reward and recognition. As an example, in one company, departments even invited the other departments over for an open house. This is where they got to show off their efforts and share best practices with other groups. This helps spread the word and makes lean infectious throughout the company.

6

Kaizen Event Examples

The authors decided to include this chapter in the book to provide selected examples of specific kaizen events based on their extensive experience performing kaizens. The rationale behind showing what other teams have accomplished is to allow you, the reader, to gain from their experience and lessons learned. Why reinvent the wheel if you can gain some insights based on what others have done?

There are many ways to perform kaizen events; the methods presented in this section may be considered typical. The point is not necessarily to replicate what these other teams have done, but to shed some light on how teams improved their processes.

A wise lean champion once said to one of the authors, "I will show you everything we've done, but please do not repeat it." Thinking that there was some proprietary information or that he really didn't want to share his techniques, the author questioned why the lean champion didn't want his results to be replicated. His response was, "Because you would be just repeating our mistakes. We have already learned how to improve what I have shown you. Learn how to make it better for your organization, in your own way."

These examples were chosen because they represent a wide range of kaizen applications, everything from classic kaizen events like 5S or quick changeover all the way to nontraditional applications like improving areas in the office or support functions. These examples also encompass a wide variety of industries and geographical locations. Selected kaizen events that are presented in this chapter include:

- 5S workplace organization and standardization

- Accounting (credits)

- Cell design

- Layout

- Request for quote to order entry

- Quick changeover

- Shipping, delivery, and logistics

- Standard work in customer service

- TPM

- Value stream mapping (from request for quote to delivery)

- Visual workplace

5S WORKPLACE ORGANIZATION AND STANDARDIZATION

Background

5S is about workplace organization and standardization and is considered a fundamental building block of lean. A practical way to perform a 5S event is to break it into its elements in a train–do mode. This means to have the team learn about "sort" and then go perform "sort" in the target area. Then proceed on to set in order and so on. This section gives an example of a 5S kaizen. For more information, see Appendix B.

The Kaizen Event

Out of all the 5S events that we have worked on, this one was unique in how the team was able to change the scope of its project based on information gathered for the current state. Performing 5S in a quick kaizen is a very common and effective way to deploy 5S throughout an organization. This is also an example of how 5S can be performed in an office or support function setting. In this particular event, one of the main goals was originally going to focus on the level of quality in the department (also known as first-pass yield or FPY). After reviewing information relating to the current state, the team made a breakthrough decision that it should start with the basic lean concept of 5S combined with visual workplace, POUS, and one-point lessons.

Originally the project was selected based on information gathered from the VSM. The team used several tools to collect information regarding its current state. The team reviewed the current state map, used spaghetti diagrams (the department was recently rearranged by the manager, *not* by a lean team), drew process flow diagrams, created a cause-and-effect diagram, reviewed current procedures, interviewed workers, and performed personal observations.

At this juncture is when the critical step was taken to change the event from focusing on quality and to move to the more basic lean concept of 5S. Team consensus was used because it was obvious to the team members that this would have the biggest impact to daily production and set the tone for future improvements.

The team consisted of the department manager, supervisor, five people from the two affected departments, two customer service representatives (internal customers and suppliers), a lean champion, and a facilitator. The team's original goals for the project would still be improved by performing 5S. The original measurable goals were:

- Improve accuracy

- Increase throughput

- Simplify the process

- Prevent passing defects on to the next operation

The new layout was performed because there were two departments that were consecutive steps in the process but were physically located in separate buildings. The new layout allowed these two groups to be located next to each other in adjacent rooms. There were many new challenges, including communication issues, streamlining the process handoffs, and completing the move. Also, there was a massive backlog of work. Customer service representatives didn't trust the department to get the work done on time or thought the department would physically lose the paperwork. Since the move was recent, this provided the team an opportune time to implement 5S from the start.

Once the team members realized that the scope of the project changed, they brainstormed opportunities for improvement, gathered as many supplies as possible, enlisted help from other departments, and dug into their work. The team came up with 77 ideas for improvement and broke them down into the following categories: schedule, communication, organize, technology, 5S, training, and safety. The team focused on specific tasks including organizing a drop-off area and arranging and labeling cabinets, files, and tables.

The drop-off table was an area where the customer service representatives dropped off and logged in their material for the next department to perform its operations. Unfortunately, prior to the event the table became covered with work in process. This made it extremely difficult for the department to maintain control over its work and first-in first-out (FIFO)

A Simple Example of Overprocessing Waste

While reviewing the steps that the operators performed, it was noted that a three-part form was used. The original form was filled in by a customer service representative and taken to the next department. In the next step, the information was logged into a hand-written tracking system. The operator then made a *copy* of the form and gave the top sheet back to the customer service representative. Whenever a copy is made, there is a high probability that it may be a type of waste known as overprocessing (doing more than the customer wants or needs).

At first, the simple fix seems to replace the three-part form with a four-part form. This would eliminate the need to make a copy of the form. Before jumping to conclusions or doing the quick fix, though, the facilitator challenged the team to gather more information to determine why this is being done.

When the operators were asked why they made a copy of a three-part form, they replied, "Because we need to keep a copy and the next department never returns our copy of the form."

When operators in the next department were interviewed, the team discovered that they too made a copy of the form! When the facilitator asked if they could return the forms to the other department, they said, "yes," which eliminated the need for either department to make any copies of the form.

Lessons learned: look for waste, determine why there is waste, eliminate it, and communicate!

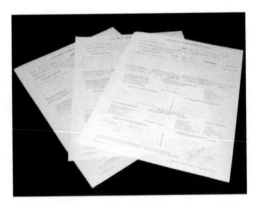

operations, and to keep track of important items and due dates. The customer service representatives created their own methods and work-arounds to make sure that their materials were visible in the pile. See Sidebar 6.1 for a simple example of overprocessing waste.

The team came up with a new methodology to log in materials and maintain orderliness of the log-in table. See Figure 6.1. The departments worked together to determine the best method to get this done. After testing it out, they used visual controls (signs, lines, labels, and color coding) and created a one-point lesson to show how to correctly perform the new procedure.

Part of the team worked on arranging cabinets and files. This included determining what was needed in the area (POUS). The team used the first three steps in 5S (sort, set in order, and shine) to make this happen.

A simple question to keep the team focused on the improvement was to ask, "Where do you use this and how often?" "Where do you use this?" helps determine where it should be located. This can reduce walking or

---

One-Page Summary

Problem: Log-in table not organized.

Before	After

Solution: Performed 5S

Benefit: More visual, less searching time, reduced chance of anything being lost

The lean team wishes to thank Maria and Nancy
for their help and assistance.

Figure 6.1   Log-in table one-page summary.

motion waste. Asking, "How often do you use this?" will help determine if it needs to be stored nearby or farther away. If it is used every day, it should be as close to the operator as possible (without getting in the way, of course!). If it is used only once a month, it can be stored farther away, but still accessible to the user.

The team also used simple visual controls to improve the work area. Since many people came in and out of the department (and since the layout was new) it was important to use visual controls to help everyone get their tasks done as quickly and easily as possible. Color coding was also employed to determine the status of work and the reason why it wasn't complete. This helped the operators and management determine where the WIP was and the reasons for quality issues. See Figure 6.2. The team also added

One-Point Lesson

On-hold reason codes

Put color clip on folder to match on-hold reason code.

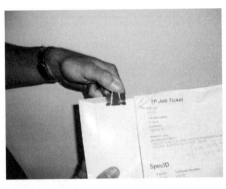

Reason	Color	
Missing files	Blue	
No purchase order	Green	
Type or copy change	Red	
Information not clear	Yellow	
Other	White	

Figure 6.2 One-point lesson for determining on-hold codes.

a communication board in an area where most of the employees would pass by sometime during the workday. This allowed the supervisor to communicate important information across all shifts in a timely manner. See Figure 6.3. Cabinets were reorganized and labeled and contents were posted on the outside. This reduced the search time for items and made it much easier to reorder supplies when needed. See Figure 6.4. Work tables were cleaned up, supplies were positioned for ease of use, and set in order was applied. See Figure 6.5.

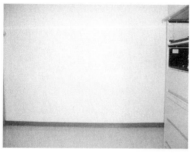

Before: an empty wall   After: communication board installed

Figure 6.3   Before and after photos of communication board.

Before   After

Figure 6.4   Before and after photos of cabinets.

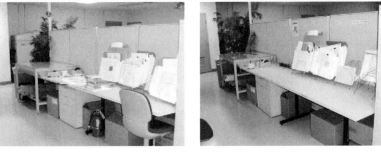

Before   After

A place for everything and
everything in its place.

Figure 6.5 Before and after photos of work tables.

Benefits

When following up with the project a few weeks after the original event, the facilitator visited the work area and spoke with operators and people from the customer service department. It was apparent the effort had sustained itself since there were no items out of place. The team had worked on the 30-day action item list and continued its efforts. The supervisor was happy because the backlog of work was completely gone. The operators liked the new method because it was simple and easy. It was visually apparent where everything belonged and the status of the work. One of the most pleasing and unexpected benefits was that it reduced the operators' and customer service representatives' stress levels! Everyone commented on how it was much better, work was being completed on time, and no materials were lost any more!

ACCOUNTING—CREDITS

Background

This organization wanted to improve its credit issuing process. A typical reason a credit may have to be issued is because an invoice or bill doesn't match what the customer owes. This can become a very complicated issue for many companies. In this particular case, there were several reasons why this had to be addressed. The top issues were:

- In the company's customer satisfaction survey, credit issues were in the top five dissatisfiers for the last four years

- The company was issuing too many credits, worth millions of dollars

- Customers wouldn't pay their invoices until the credit issue was resolved, which affected cash flow

- It took up to three weeks to get a credit issue resolved

The team consisted of a sponsor, a change agent, two customer service representatives, a credit manager, a data integrity specialist, a quality technician, a Six Sigma Black Belt, a sales representative, a corporate training coordinator, and an outside facilitator.

The Kaizen Event

The team decided that the purpose of the kaizen event was "to better understand credit issues and provide lean learning to office associates." The scope was to focus on general office wastes and credit note process clarification. There were three goals for the event:

1. Resolve customer issues in less than three days

2. Institute physical changes to remove waste

3. Analyze top three credit customers and freight issues

As part of understanding the current state, the team created a process-level VSM, as shown in Figure 6.6. This map focused on invoicing and issuing credits. The team split into two groups in order to save time developing the map. One of the biggest benefits of performing the walk-through while creating the VSM was that everyone was able to finally see the entire process. This also allowed team members to identify waste in the system. On another note, in this map the team used only one process box (out of 24) to

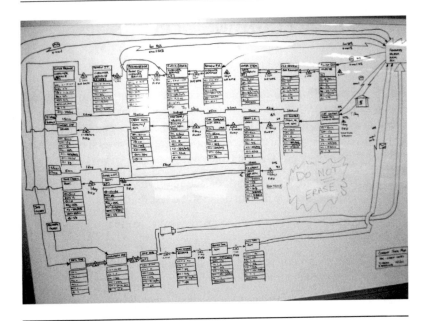

Figure 6.6   Credits VSM.

designate manufacturing. This showed the team how complicated its support function systems were.

During the walk-through and by giving the team time to determine the current state, the team members were able to use the eight wastes of lean to identify opportunities for improvement. Some of the general comments included:

- Slow process = backlog of credits.

- There is no clear process.

- There is no idea of the big picture.

- There is an inability to capture and transfer institutional knowledge.

- We are unaware of the impact of freight issues.

Overproduction

- We go through invoices one at a time. Some are fixed and then reprinted.

- Documents (invoices and so on) are printed and not collected for weeks. See Figure 6.7.

Figure 6.7   Backlog of credits.

Motion

- Invoices and credits are printed at a remote printer.
- People with similar jobs sit in different work areas.

Waiting

- People wait for credit information.
- We spend eight hours printing, folding, and stuffing envelopes.
- There is inefficient office equipment.

Defects

- Incorrect information is passed along to the next internal customer.

Overprocessing

- Credits were reviewed by multiple people in the credit stream.

The team came up with 53 ideas for improvement to the process. The team was split into groups to implement the ideas that were doable in a short period of time. The rest of the items were placed on the 30-day action item list for the change agent to monitor. The team used the following building blocks of lean to improve the process:

- *Visual controls.* Team members placed labels on office equipment indicating whom to contact if any maintenance was needed. For instance, "If there is a problem, call Joe Smith in the IT department at extension 467." They also created one-point lessons for several pieces of the office equipment and other processing steps.

- *5S and POUS.* Unneeded items were red tagged and items that needed repair or replacement were identified. In order to reduce motion waste (walking), the team decided to move the high-volume printer to a better location closer to the point of use.

- *Teams and teamwork.* Even though there had been training on a new method to get low-cost credits through the system, not everyone was following the process they dubbed "fast track." After talking with the customer service representatives, the team decided that they needed additional training, so it put together a new session and held it during the kaizen event.

During the current state data analysis, the team discovered that two significant reasons for the credit issues (freight charges and sales/software issues) were beyond the scope of this project, so it decided to spin off two separate teams to address these issues.

- *VSM.* By having the process-level VSM, people were finally able to see the complexity of their system. By using the current state map they were able to identify additional opportunities for improvement. The change agent was placed in charge of updating the map and communicating the progress of the action items. By calculating the rolled throughput yield (RTY) from the beginning of the process to the end, the team discovered that there was only a seven percent chance that an invoice would make it through the system correctly the first time.

- *Standard work.* The team decided to create several one-point lessons to show and train people how to perform tasks in the customer service area. These one-point lessons were simple, visual, and easy to understand. The one-point lessons that were related to office equipment were placed at the equipment so that anyone using the machine knew how to operate it. Standard work sheets were used to train the customer service representatives and account executives on the fast-track system.

- *Layout.* By using the spaghetti diagrams, the team was able to discover that a new office layout would be beneficial. Some of the people doing the same tasks were located in another part of the office. Also, there was no clear flow or line of sight between the internal supplier and customer. See Figure 6.8.

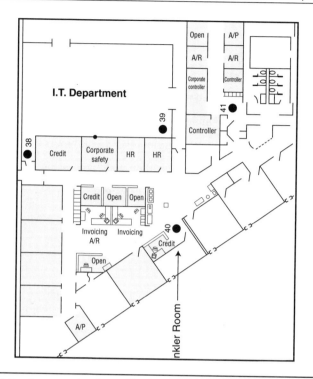

Figure 6.8 An example of an office layout.

• *Poka-yoke (error-proofing).* The team decided that it needed to work with the information technology department to error-proof defaults on some of the computer screens.

The final outcomes were broken into three main projects:

1. Freight credits

   • Team formed to resolve freight credit issues

   • Team identified and created one-point lessons to help simplify processes

   • Team identified top three customers with the most freight credits and developed a plan of attack

2. Physical changes

   • Team recommended a more efficient office layout

- Team identified office equipment for removal or repair
- Team identified and created one-point lessons to help simplify processes
- Team recommended purchase of new office equipment

3. Fast-track process improvement

   - Improvement resulted in a smoother credit process
   - Improvement increased speed of credit processing
   - Processes were put in place to measure results
   - Team identified and created one-point lessons to help simplify processes

Benefits

The kaizen event produced both quantitative and qualitative results. The quantitative results were:

- Reduced the time required to process credits. See Table 6.1.
- Reduced the time required for handling invoices. See Table 6.2.
- Created one-point lessons for freight to reduce errors in shipping.

The qualitative results were:

- Editable PDF fast-track form
- Reduced frustration with credit process
- Created one-point lessons to clear up confusion
- Financial results
- Reduced cost of processing credits

Table 6.1   Kaizen event goals.

	Before	**After**
Time to process fast track	6 days	3 days
Time to process invoices	48 hours	24 hours
Freight errors	396 freight-related credits YTD	50% reduction

Table 6.2 Kaizen event metrics.

Item	Before	Goal	Actual	Improvement
Fast track response time	6 days	< 3 days	2.3 days	Greater than 50% savings in lead time
Physical changes	Motion waste	Minimize motion	Office layout changed	Reduced walking distances
Freight credits	396/3000 13%	200 6.5%	214	Long-term goal— no credits related to freight
Top three credit customers	No idea of where freight credits were from	Identified customers	25% of freight issues originated from three customers	Team formed to focus on reasons and outline plan

- Potential reduction in freight credits
- Reduced non-value-added functions

Future action items included a list of over 100 ideas to improve the credit process.

CELL DESIGN

Background

This kaizen event was not a traditional assembly cell, but rather a cellular and flow design that focused on eliminating waste in a bottleneck area. This process was in the finishing department of a company and was the last step before shipping. Employees called this area a cell, but after simple observation it was easy to determine that it was not actually a cell, but a moderately good layout to get machines closer together. One of the telltale signs that it was not a true cell was the amount of batching between process steps and that the process was not line-balanced for optimal flow.

Not all the products went through this step, but volumes had steadily increased (and were expected to continue to increase), causing the bottleneck. The main processing steps were to cut, inspect, shrink-wrap, and package the product. There were two work centers that could perform this task, but the cutting machines were different and had a constraint on the sizes they could cut (large and small).

The team followed a five-step process for developing a work cell:

1. Determine the process family

2. Calculate the takt time

3. Review the standard work

4. Balance the work flow

5. Create the cell

How to conduct the full implementation of a cell is beyond the scope of this book, but many of the steps and processes are mentioned in this section.

Prior to this project, the company created a VSM that included changing this step into more of a flow process or cell. The company had already started a 5S program and was using QCO on other equipment. This project was picked because of the bottleneck situation, and the team wanted to make sure that it could have a "win" to show others that these lean concepts actually work.

The team consisted of the area manager, a lead person, an operator, a helper, a member of production control, the second shift superintendent as the project leader, and a facilitator. For this particular event, a member of maintenance was unable to attend due to personnel issues and resources (the team recognized this ahead of time and didn't want this to delay the improvements). This type of situation is not altogether unusual in kaizen events. Two of the team members had participated in lean training or prior kaizen events; the others were new to lean. Most of the employees in this area had been with the company for many years.

The team determined the following goals for the project:

- Improve flow

- Increase throughput

- Reduce search time

- Avoid feast-or-famine routine; level the schedule

- Be flexible for growth, create extra capacity

- Standardize more

- Become better organized

- Ensure better quality

- Reduce changeover times

- Improve safety

- Reduce WIP

- Reduce stress

- Make better use of floor space

- Reduce motion and transportation wastes

Current State

In order to understand the current state, the team used several methods to document the as-is situation, including recording the target area information, a process-level VSM, spaghetti diagrams, process flow diagrams, productivity and capacity analysis, photographs, and time observations. The team also took measurements and updated the current floor plan.

Determining the target area information was enlightening for the team members because they agreed that there were 23 different functions being performed in the area. It was easy to identify what the basic steps were, but they also realized that they performed other functions in that area like paperwork, preventive maintenance, setups, quality approvals, and moving product. These simple items tend to get overlooked in preference to the actual production process. They also identified over 25 pieces of equipment and tools used in the area.

The process-level VSM was used to show the flow (or lack thereof) for the two production lines. By using the VSM, the team determined that 10.5 percent of its time was value-added. It was a good basis from which to determine some of the other things that the team needed to work on in the future to eliminate more waste. The spaghetti diagrams showed that on an average day the operators walked over three miles getting the next job, performing a setup, performing the work, doing paperwork, and getting and moving materials. See Figure 6.9.

One of the key elements of the process flow diagrams showed that many of the steps (18 out of 22!) were just to set up the job and to close it out. This finding helped tremendously when the team looked at the productivity and capacity analysis. With the average number of setups taken into consideration, the operators were spending approximately three hours a day in setting up jobs and closing them out.

Another major breakthrough while performing this analysis showed the unevenness of the schedule. This function would be light on work for two days and then get swamped with work for the next four. This inconsistency

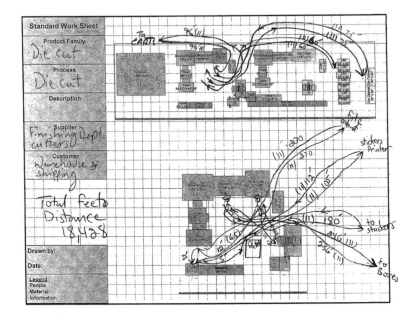

Figure 6.9   Spaghetti diagram—cell.

added to overtime and working weekends. Sharing this information with the production control person made her realize that she needed to feed work to this function in a steady, more consistent manner (level loading). The photos showed the current conditions, including the need for more 5S and general disarray of materials that added to the search time. Team members understood that they needed to perform time observations on the tasks so that they would be better able to line-balance the operation.

To help team members understand the lean concept of how batch-size reduction actually improves a process, they participated in a short exercise that illustrates this point. See Sidebar 6.2. The concept of batch-size reduction seemed counterintuitive to the operators: "How can I be more efficient by making only one at a time?" The team decided that it would put a maximum of five kanban squares on the transfer table after cutting and before shrink-wrapping. If the kanbans were full, the cutting operator was to stop and help final pack-out.

Batch-Size Reduction Exercise

Purpose: To show the concept of how batch-size reduction:

- Can improve production by reducing lead time

- Can get the first item completed faster

- Can identify defects quicker

Scope:

- Can be performed with a minimum number of people (recommend no less than three participants)

- Requires about 10 to 15 minutes to perform with a report-out

Setup: This can be either run by having the same size teams compete against each other or, if it is a small group, run the exercise in two to three rounds.

- The teams can sit next to each other, but it is not required. If they are not sitting next to each other, it is recommended to number each workstation so they know where the cards go next.

- If using multiple teams (2 or 3), have one team perform the task in full batch mode of 10. Have the other team(s) perform in batches of five or one.

- If using one group, have it repeat the exercise for batches of 10, five, and/or one).

- Tell the team(s) that they have four orders of 10 cards each (for a total of 40 cards). Each order of 10 cards is a different color. This shows how batching moves through a system more realistically (multiple orders versus only one order).

- Tell the batching groups that they can only move their stacks when their batch is completely done. No moving partial batches.

Continued

Continued

- Tell the team that the following information will be tracked:

  - First piece complete

  - Entire order complete

  - Entire production run complete

  - Defect detected

Items needed:

- 3" × 5" assorted colors index cards (minimum of four colors, 10 cards each color per team per round)

- A pen for each participant

- A stopwatch or the second hand on a watch

- A place to record the results

Exercise:

- Tell team members that they are to print their full names on the index cards (this is their process step). Since each person has a different length name and it takes a different amount of time to print their full name, this shows that batch-size reduction even works when the line isn't balanced or cycle times are different.

- The team that does batches of 10 (or five) has to wait until the entire batch of 10 (or five) is complete before it can move the cards to the next person.

- The group that does batch size of one (make one, move one) can pass an index card to the next person as soon as they are finished printing their full name on it.

- Have the cards start in one location and finish in another location

- Record the times it takes to get the first card through, the first order of 10 through, and the entire production of four orders. Use a table like the one following:

Continued

Item	Team 1	Team 2	Team 3
First piece off			
First order complete			
Entire production complete			
Defect detection			

Report-out

- Even though the teams worked as fast as they could, the batch size of 10 takes the longest because of the lack of flow.

- Ask the teams how they felt (the human side of lean). Some may say "rushed" or "under pressure."

- Talk about how long it would take for the next operation to find a defect. For instance if the team uses batch sizes of 10, it may take a while before the next operation finds the defect. But the team that performs in batch sizes of one would find the same defect in a very short period of time. Ask them which one would be better.

- Change the times from minutes/seconds to days or weeks and ask the teams from whom they would rather purchase (based on the times) for the first piece off (the equivalent of "I need one right away!"), the entire order, or how long before they find a defect.

Cellular Design Five-Step Process

The process families (also known as product families) were determined during the original value stream mapping event. The team calculated the takt time by taking the time available per shift and dividing it by the demand (per shift). One of the key things that the team had to work through was that the two main pieces of equipment for each cell had different change-over times and different demands (based on the physical size of the product). Separate takt times were calculated for each cell along with takt times based on the minimum, average, and maximum demand. See Table 6.3.

Table 6.3   Takt time example.

Time available		Minutes
Shift		480
Breaks		−10
Lunch		−20
5S		−10
Meetings		−5
Changeover		−220
Maintenance		−5
Other		−0
Total minutes		210
Total seconds		12,600
Demand	Min	900
	Avg	1,080
	Max	1,800
Takt time (Min) =		12,600 900
Takt time (Avg) =		12,600 1080
Takt time (Max) =		12,600 1800
Takt time	Min	14.0
	Avg	11.7
	Max	7.0

Since this work area did not have any standard work previously, the team had to perform time observations and create standard work combination sheets. The team was split into two groups and each group took different portions of the process. If a particular step wasn't being performed, team members either did it themselves or waited for the other crew to work on it. They looked at cyclic and noncyclic steps. See Figure 6.10.

When performing the line balancing, the focus wasn't as much on the process steps since they were relatively simple and not very time-consuming. The key here was to put kanban squares in place so that the cutting operator did not overproduce and swamp the next operator. The real benefit was to balance the times during the setup and closeout. One of the biggest

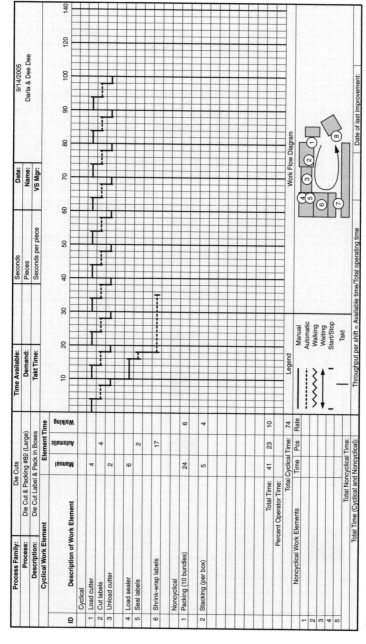

Figure 6.10 Standard work combination sheet.

breakthroughs occurred when the team discovered that a step performed during setup could be performed by another department that had extra capacity, without having any deleterious effect. This freed the helper to lend a hand to the operator to perform more of the changeover tasks. See Figure 6.11.

Creating the actual layout is the last step. Beware! Many people want to start with this step, because it may seem the most fun or exciting. Do not do this. Without knowing the actual current state conditions and following the five-step process, you may end up doing more harm than good. The team used scale drawings of the area with magnets and a magnetic board to try different layouts. By having the team look at it from different angles and perspectives, there were 10 major revisions while going through this step (including adding another piece of equipment that was not currently in the cell). The team also determined that it would have to create the cell in two phases because of the need for support from the maintenance department and other outside resources. Phase I was what they could change during the

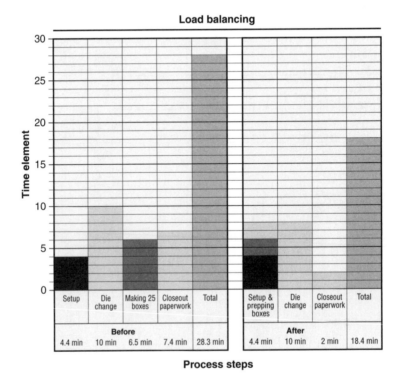

Figure 6.11   Load balancing chart.

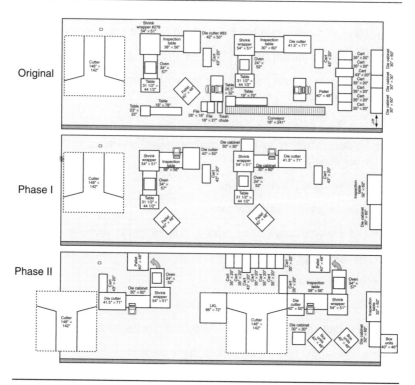

Figure 6.12 Layouts.

actual kaizen event. Phase II required changes in electrical, riggers, and adding another large piece of equipment. See Figure 6.12.

The team came up with 35 additional ideas to improve the work area and placed them on its 30-day action item list to make sure that they were completed. After carrying out the five-step process, the team went to the work area and performed the first three steps of 5S, sort, set in order, and shine, by removing items that weren't needed, deciding where the needed items would go, and cleaning the area. Next, team members set the equipment in the proper location according to Phase I of their plan. They spent time on visual controls including signs, lines, labels, and color coding items.

Results

By performing 5S and redesigning the cell, the team was able to reduce the square footage needed from almost 1400 square feet to less than 1000 square feet while adding another (large) piece of equipment. The team came up with the following lessons learned:

- Have stopwatches on hand to perform time observations

- Don't jump ahead; follow the five-step process

- Make sure you get other people from other departments involved when needed

- Get rid of items not needed in the area

- Explore different layouts (several iterations); in this case, the team explored 10

- Conduct good brainstorming

- Have everyone contribute ideas

- Get low-cost items, like a printer, to reduce walking distance

- Be open to new ideas

- Balance the workload

- Have an outsider give other points of view

- Try multiple configurations (from a straight line to a U-shape layout)

- Look for too many unneeded items in the area

- When we work as a team we can almost accomplish the impossible

- The new layout is a very efficient design

- Action items in our area can affect other areas

- Why wait four years before we change it again!

LAYOUT

Background

This layout was performed in a laboratory that processes tests for a local hospital. The first step of the laboratory process was to log in specimens for testing. This function was performed in what they called the central processing area of the laboratory. A main goal for this facility was to be able to process more tests (continual growth is expected) with the current number of technicians. This would also free up release time for individuals to devote to continuous improvement projects (such as lean or Six Sigma) without adding staff. Since this area was the beginning of the overall process, it had a critical role for all downstream customers; it was a perfect candidate to redesign its workstations and flow.

The team comprised a cross-functional group, including staff from the area, technicians from the other departments, the business analyst, and an outside facilitator. The team determined that the scope of the project could potentially affect six additional areas. The team decided to use the lean approach of:

1. Get current layout information

2. Create new layout

3. Determine layout plan

4. Implement plan

Current State

As part of gathering information on the current state, the team came up with the general consensus of the area as being:

- Cramped

- Not flexible

- Designed to require excessive movements

- Cluttered

- Disorganized

- Not standardized

- Nonergonomic

The team used the eight wastes of lean to identify opportunities for improvement. The wastes were:

- *Overproduction.* They were producing more, earlier, and faster than the next operation could handle by batching the work because of how the work was sent to them. The line wasn't balanced.

- *Motion.* There was a lot of motion (walking) waste discovered by observing the operations, due to the location of copiers, printers, workstations, and equipment. Long workbenches required people to walk around them to get to other areas, which was not conducive to flow or teamwork. Team members created spaghetti diagrams to show motion and transportation wastes. See Figure 6.13.

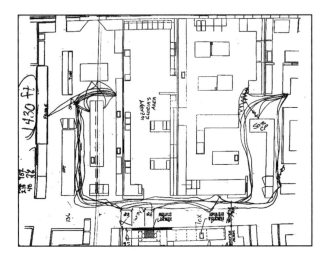

Figure 6.13 Spaghetti diagram of central processing area.

- Inventory waste was noticed due to the excess supplies that were not visual or at point of use.

- There was transportation waste because specimens were moved long distances and necessary supplies were stored farther away than they needed to be.

- Waiting waste included waiting for specimens to arrive, shift overlap created waiting for computer availability, and slow computers, printers, and so on, created delays.

- Utilization of teams was limited to PDCA model, lean tools were not previously used, and there typically were no facilitation resources.

- Defects slowed down the process because forms were not accurate and complete, labels or information were missing, and one person (instead of teams) solved problems.

- Overprocessing was identified because of excessive paperwork. See Figure 6.14.

The team determined that the main goal of the project would be to change the layout of the central processing area to improve flow and quality and to reduce the lead time for test results. Specific goals included:

- Improve the work flow in central processing

- Communicate better within departments and between departments, including management

- Make work environment better

- Keep area clean and organized by rigorous application of 5S principles

- Stay within constraints

- Be flexible for future considerations

The team used several tools to help determine the current state, including creating a process family matrix, process flow diagrams, spaghetti diagrams, takt time, photographs, and interviewing others not on the layout team. Input from those not on the layout team provided several benefits. First of all, it helped to build buy-in. Because of the size limitation for effectiveness of teams (about seven to 10 people), it was not always possible to have everyone in a department participate in the kaizen event. A way to circumvent this situation was to allow the team to perform interviews with people not included on the team. This is an extremely effective method to help reduce the fear of change or fear of the unknown. It is also a perfect way to gather good ideas for the project.

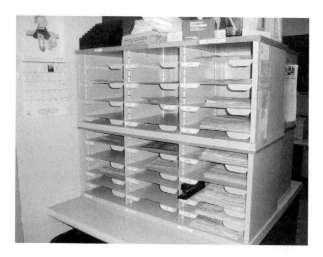

Figure 6.14 Excessive paperwork.

Guidelines that will help participants perform the interviews for maximum results include having only one or two people interview a candidate. You do not want it to seem like an inquisition. If there are two interviewers, one can concentrate on asking the questions and probing when necessary and the other person can concentrate on taking notes. See Figure 6.15 for

Question	Results
How can you reduce your search time?	
What equipment do you share?	
Do you have any ergonomic issues?	
How could we make your stock system more visual?	
How can you move around your work area easily?	
How can we document best practices or lessons learned?	
How can we improve communication?	
How could we improve having the work instructions at the point of use?	
How could we incorporate a planned maintenance system?	
How could we use shadow boards for tools at the workstations?	
How could we better organize the tools?	
Where and how could we use color coding?	
Where and how could we post metrics (for example, quality issues, rates, and schedules) for the department?	
How could we use visual signals to show status of repairs?	
How could we improve the flow of materials through the department?	
How could we improve the trash removal?	
How could we use error-proofing?	
How could we ensure tool recall?	
How could we communicate takt time?	
How could we improve the specific flow of materials at your workstation?	

Figure 6.15 Example of a layout interview form.

an example of a layout interview form. Tell the interviewees that their responses will be anonymous if they feel uncomfortable. Put the interviewee at ease. Also, mention that not all ideas may be incorporated into the layout based on the constraints of the project. Good ideas not implemented at this time will be put on a future action item list so that they are not lost or forgotten.

Implementation

Because of construction and other changes in the lab, the team had time to prepare for the actual physical changes. A major benefit of changing the layout was that the team was able to add additional workstations. The original setup had long workbenches. The new layout had a breakthrough concept of moving work tables into groups of three, or "pods." This improved flow and, more importantly for the team, induced better communication. Because the team took time to analyze the information it gathered (process flow diagrams, spaghetti diagrams, data analysis), it had realized that 40 percent of the specimens had to flow to one area first, and the remaining 60 percent went to another area. The team created a layout that would allow the bulk of the material to flow through the center of the department. The layout team also worked with the 5S team to standardize the workstations. See Figures 6.16 and 6.17.

At first there was resistance from the technicians to making each workstation the same. Team members took time with each technician to explain the reasoning behind the standardization of the workstations and

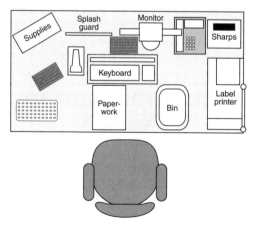

Figure 6.16 A standardized workstation.

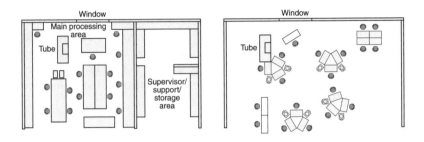

Figure 6.17   A layout of the work area before applying lean (left) and after (right).

the benefits. They also took suggestions from the technicians who were not originally on the team, which helped build buy-in from all those who would work in the area. The results of the implementation included:

- Improved flow

- Minimized motion and transportation wastes

- Better organization

- Effective communication

- A team approach

- More visual, line-of-sight materials

- Gained more work area

- Consideration for future changes

In order to better prepare for either layout events or cell design, Table 6.4 is a checklist of items and supplies that may be useful.

REQUEST FOR QUOTE TO ORDER ENTRY

Background

Request for quote (RFQ) forms were taking too long to process, even though the company had an informal policy of turning them around as soon as possible, but at least the time was in line with competitors. Many times estimators guessed what the customer really wanted when information on

Table 6.4   A sample cellular/flow pre-event checklist.

Area/☑	Item	Quantity	Notes
Training room			
	LCD projector	1	
	Screen	1	
	Laptop	1	
	Flip chart	1	
	Markers	4	Black, blue, red, green
	Large sticky notes		
	Medium-size permanent markers		
	Masking tape	1	Roll
	Pens, pencils, and erasers		Enough for each team
	Clipboards		One for every person
	Rulers		
	Digital camera	1	
	Notepads		
	Breakfast/lunch menu		TBD during planning phase
	Scissors		
Layout/cell			
	Scale drawing of work area	4	With current equipment
	Scale drawing of work area	4	*Without* current equipment
	Stopwatches		One per team
	Time observation sheet		
	Standard work combination sheet		
	Standard work sheet		
	Work capacity table		
	Loading chart		
	One-point lesson form		
	Spaghetti diagram		
	Magnets		
	Magnetic board		
	Double-sided tape	1 roll	
Other			
	Current procedure(s)		From target area

the RFQ was incomplete or unclear. Not following up with customers in a timely fashion frequently led to losing the job to a competitor. The hit rate on bids was not at an acceptable level and was slipping.

The kaizen team comprised two people from customer service, one from sales, one from order entry, one from estimating, one from manufacturing engineering, one industrial engineer, one supervisor, and the external facilitator. The team used the following kaizen tools: process mapping and value stream mapping, supplier–inputs–process–outputs–customer (SIPOC) linkages and handoffs, spaghetti diagrams, brainstorming, check sheets, benchmarking, root cause analysis tools, Pareto charts, Gantt charts, training in the eight wastes, and the lean building blocks.

The team's goals were to:

- Form a team, train, and collect data

- Generate the process map first, then the VSM

- Create a spaghetti diagram based on approximate walking involved in the office by the people involved in the RFQ to order entry process

- Identify the eight wastes of lean in the process under study and the appropriate building block as the solution

- Use root cause analysis tools to determine various forms of waste

- Brainstorm, build consensus, and rank improvement opportunities

- Set goals for the improved future state

- Implement the agreed-upon improvement plan

- Monitor, analyze, and tweak, if necessary, the results

- Create the 30-day action item list

- Standardize at the improved level

- Present to management

Current State

The kaizen team identified the current situation as follows:

- Work spaces are cluttered.

- Some of the required information is stored away in distant file cabinets.

- RFQs coming in through faxes or in the mail get routed to the wrong person, thus causing delay (or some even get lost).

- Too many reviews and approvals cause delays and waiting.

- The personnel working in the RFQ to order entry process in the company do not fully understand value-added versus non-value-added tasks/time.

- Physical files and paperwork move in a zigzag fashion.

- Every RFQ is treated the same way (the same importance is given to each). The in-boxes and out-boxes are not immediately clear to others.

- Printers, fax machines, and other office equipment sometimes break down, run out of toner, need paper, and so on.

- There are delays due to people being sick, on vacation, or away from the office. Also, at other times an important customer sends in a large batch of RFQs all at once.

- Sometimes in-process RFQs sit in out- or in-boxes in batches.

- Required follow-up with customers is not done (or is not done on time).

- Sometimes similar RFQs are grouped together for processing, which results in some urgent bids getting delayed.

The average turnaround time for an RFQ was 12 working days. Comparing this lead time with value-adding time, the kaizen team discovered that 96 percent of the lead time was non-value-added. The flowchart in Figure 6.18 identifies the processing steps.

The company did not want to include the following items in the scope of this kaizen: credit check of new customers, in-house capacity/inventory check, direct purchase orders from customers (without going through the quote process), and orders for finished goods inventory (stock) items.

The facilitator had the team identify the wastes, which included waiting, defects, overprocessing, motion, and underutilized people. Then the team brainstormed about which lean building block to use for each type of waste or bottleneck. See Table 6.5.

The future state goal was to reduce the lead time in turning around a quote from the typical 12 working days to one day. The kaizen team achieved outstanding results. By implementing the solutions identified, the lead time was cut to one day, so that an RFQ could be processed and a

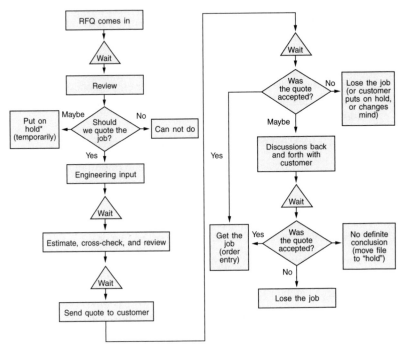

*Need more information from customer, need the standards/specifications, need specific information from subcontractors or from manufacturing engineering.

Figure 6.18　RFQ flowchart.

quote transmitted to the customer (or customer was informed of "Regret—no quote") within 24 hours. The company was able to increase the service level to its customers and scored higher on customer satisfaction surveys. This, in turn, improved its hit rate as well as increased sales.

QUICK CHANGEOVER

Background

This project was a changeover kaizen event on a printing press. In the printing industry, this is commonly known as a makeready. At the time of this event there were about 40 employees in this facility over two shifts. One month prior to the QCO event, the entire facility received one-day lean overview training. This project was chosen from the company's VSM and was based on the impact it would have on the process and people.

Table 6.5 Wastes and lean building block solutions.

No.	Waste	Building block solution
1	Work spaces are cluttered.	5S
2	Some of the required information is stored away in distant file cabinets.	POUS
3	RFQ coming in through faxes or in the mail get routed to the wrong person, thus causing delay (or some even get lost).	Standard work
4	Too many reviews and approvals cause delays and waiting.	Quality at the source
5	The personnel working in the RFQ to order entry process in the company do not fully understand value-added versus non-value-added tasks/time.	VSM
6	Physical files and paperwork move in a zigzag fashion	Layout
7	Every RFQ is treated the same way (the same importance is given to each). The in-boxes and out-boxes are not immediately clear to others.	Visual workplace
8	Printers, fax machines, and other office equipment sometimes break down, run out of toner, need the right paper, and so on.	Office TPM
9	There are delays due to people being sick, on vacation, or away from the office. Also, at other times an important customer sends in a large batch of RFQs all at once.	Teams and teamwork
10	Sometimes in-process RFQs sit in out- or in-boxes in batches.	Batch-size reduction
11	Required follow-up with customers is not done (or is not done on time).	Standard work
12	Sometimes similar RFQs are grouped together for processing, which results in some urgent bids getting delayed.	Cell layout

The cross-functional team included the following members: the printing manager, the lead pressman, an assistant pressman, a helper, the continuous improvement coordinator (who was also a Six Sigma Black Belt), three operators from other areas, and a facilitator.

Current State

In order to determine the actual current state, team members agreed to videotape a setup so they could break it down and analyze it for improvement. They had two video cameras: one for a large area view and one for a closer view of the action. In preparation for the videotaping, the scheduler made sure that a typical job was to be run next. Everyone was informed ahead of time that the team was going to videotape the process. The facilitator mentioned to the team to be aware of the Hawthorne effect while videotaping, meaning that the operators might act differently because there were observers in the area. It is not uncommon for people to either work faster when they are first videotaped because they want to show their best effort or go slower because they don't want to make any mistakes. The team also made sure that everyone knew the definition of *changeover,* which is "the time from the last good piece of the current run to the next good piece of the next run." In the printing process this includes "getting in register" and color matching.

Team members volunteered for specific roles during the videotaping. There was a camera person and assistant assigned to the two cameras, one team member drew a spaghetti diagram for the lead operator, and everyone else was given a worksheet to record their observations, including any waste that they saw and possible fixes. A digital camera was used to take photos of waste in the area and of the setup.

After the setup was complete, the team members thanked the operators performing the changeover and set off to analyze what they saw. The team reviewed the videotape and broke it down into individual steps including internal and external time or steps. Internal steps are those performed when the machine is stopped. Think of it this way—if I have my hand inside the machine, the machine better be stopped! External steps are those performed while the machine is running.

Team members watched the video and broke it down to each step using a changeover analysis chart. The chart included the following information: the step number, elapsed time, element time, internal or external time, comments, and the category of the step (process, storage, transportation, or inspection). The setup took three hours and 14 minutes. The steps and time elements were cut and pasted into a changeover observation chart to show graphically the individual time elements. See Figure 6.19 for an example of a changeover observation chart. This helped the team to focus on ways to reduce the operations that take a long time. The team noticed that there

Changeover Observation Chart

	Quick changeover		Date: X/XX/XX		Name(s): David, Derrick, Randy, Tim	Shift: 1st

Seq No.	Element	Elapsed Time	Element Time
1	Stop machine	12:31:50	
2	Filter out ink	12:32:12	0:00:22
3	Lower pans—unit 2, drain	12:32:17	0:00:27
4	Drain unit 2	12:32:59	0:00:42
5	Remove applicator holder 3	12:32:29	0:00:14
6	Back off dr blade, drain unit 3	12:33:08	0:00:39
7	Tell DJ to start unit 4	12:32:40	0:00:11
8	Remove applicator 4	12:33:00	0:00:20
9	Lower pans, back off dr blade—unit 4, drain	12:33:27	0:00:27
10	Back off dr blade 2	12:33:01	0:00:02
11	Get solvent/rag, clean cylinder 2	12:34:13	0:01:12
12	Get solvent/rag	12:33:44	0:00:17
13	Disconnect pump 5	12:33:50	0:00:06
14	Disconnect pump 6	12:33:55	0:00:06
15	Disconnect pump 7	12:34:03	0:00:08
16	Disconnect pump 8	12:34:08	0:00:05
17	Get rags	12:34:28	0:00:20
18	Clean cylinder 3	12:35:31	0:01:18
19	Clean cylinder 4 and get rags	12:35:45	0:01:17
20	Remove applicator 5	12:35:40	0:00:09
	Good product		

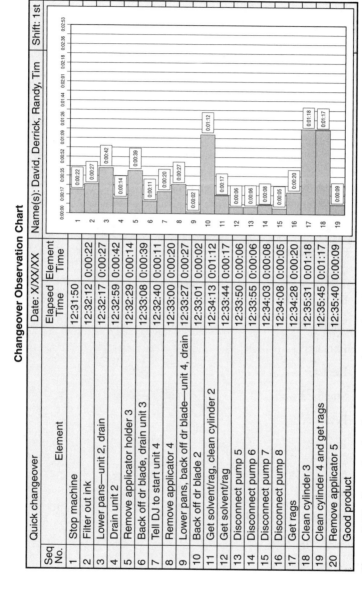

Figure 6.19 Example of a changeover observation chart.

were several times when there was no one at the machine. Operators were off looking for items, parts, people, materials, and the like. So one of the goals of the new changeover was to make sure that the machine was never unattended or not being worked on.

The team printed out the pictures and posted them on a temporary communication board placed in the area of the press. The observation and analysis charts were also posted with the spaghetti diagram. This allowed everyone to see what the current situation was. The other operators examined the information and made valuable suggestions to the team.

After reviewing the current state, the team went into the brainstorming mode. The team came up with over 120 ideas for improvement broken into 15 categories. See Figure 6.20 for an example of a 30-day action item list. The categories included:

1. Press redesign

2. Carts and storage

3. Tools

4. Doctor blades

5. Standardize

6. Benches

7. Register

8. Standard work

9. Personnel

10. Pumps

11. Communication

12. Cylinders

13. Dispensing ink and solvent

14. Cleaning

15. Visual and staging

The team then focused on the items that could be implemented during the event. Using effort and impact analysis determines which items are the best to work on and will have the biggest benefit. See Figure 5.4, page 38, to help determine which ideas to implement.

Project: Setup reduction on a makeready

Status
- O = Open 5
- C = Closed 4
- Total 9
- Complete 44%

Classification	Count	Percent
A = No assistance needed	5	55.6%
B = Other resources needed	0	0.0%
C = Management help necessary	4	44.4%
Total	9	

Classification: A = No assistance needed, B = Other resources needed, C = Management help necessary

Percent Complete: 44% / 56%

ID	Status	Classification	Priority	Description	Original completion date	Actual completion date	Assigned to (Primary)	Assigned to (Other)	Impact	Comments
				Press redesign						
1	O	A		Use new method to hold hose (no tape)			Robert	David		
2	C	A		Clip or holder for ink hose instead of taping to machine						See #1
3	O	C		Pumped white ink to press			Jim	Tim		Need to research
4	O	C		Pneumatic blade controls for doctor blades			Jim			
5	O	C		Convert Chesnut to cartridges like Rotomec			Jim			
6	O	C		Better chucks for unwind station			Jim			
				Carts and storage						
7	C	A		One cart, one deck for setup						Decided not to do at this time
8	C	A		Store pan/parts closer to press						
9	C	A		Move racks behind press for staging area						

Figure 6.20 Example of a 30-day action item list for QCO.

Implementation

The team then set out and implemented as many ideas as they could during the next two days. See Figure 6.21 to see one improved area. They also created a new procedure with expected time elements. The other operators were allowed to review the new procedure and make any suggestions for improvement. The team then went through a walk-through of the new procedure and on the last day re-videotaped the new process.

The team noticed the following qualitative results:

- Over 120 improvement ideas were generated

- The work area looks better, neater

- The work area is more organized, efficient

- There is not as much work

- There is more potential for bonuses

- Lean works for the printing industry

- Lean benefits everyone in the company

- There is higher production

- There is greater teamwork

- There is more flexibility

- There is standardization and consistency between shifts

A summary of these quantitative results appears in Table 6.6.

Figure 6.21   Photos of the workbench area before the kaizen event (left) and after (right).

Table 6.6 Results of the kaizen QCO.

Description	Before	Goal	Actual	Improvement	
Setup time (minutes)	3:14:10	1:30:00	1:36:00	51%	
Internal steps	290	150	56	81%	
External steps	0	120	60	60	estimate
Makeready footage	4,200	2,000	2,292	45%	
Walking distance (feet)	10,000	3,000	2,500	75%	estimate

Savings	Before	After	Improvement	
Changeover (minutes)	194	96	98	
Number of C/O per day	2	2		
Minutes saved per day	388	192	196	
Number of days per year	208	208		
Hours saved per year	1,345	666	679	
Per hour value	X,XXX		$ X,XXX	
Amount saved per year			$ XXX,XXX	
Investment (cost of the kaizen—estimate)			− $ 10,000	
First-year revenue			= $ XXX,XXX	

The team members decided that they wanted to brainstorm ideas to sustain their efforts so they wouldn't slip back into old habits. The following is what they came up with:

- Track changeover times (internal and external times)

- All operators will be trained the same way to use the same procedure

- Be open to new ideas

- Learn that the goal is to keep reducing changeover times

- We are a "pit crew"

- Streamline the external time tasks

- Keep everyone motivated

- Have short QCO meetings

- Reward and recognize employee efforts

- Do another kaizen event in three months

- Capture and track goals for improvement

- Have a changeover reduction design team

- Cross-train

- Do another kaizen event (like TPM) on the equipment and other areas

- Make more time for training

SHIPPING, DELIVERY, AND LOGISTICS

Current State

In this example, the kaizen team consisted of three employees from the shipping room, two truckers, one material handler, one shipping clerk, one manager, one accountant, and the external facilitator. The product was transported by truck to a central distribution warehouse, which was 900 miles away. Each truck waited at the dock during loading for an average of eight hours due to the following reasons: product to be shipped was not staged, the list of parts going into each truck or other paperwork was not ready, or product waiting to be shipped was stored all over in various locations and not always labeled or identified.

Three people worked in the shipping area. The lead was very experienced and used his memory rather than procedures, instructions, checklists, or logs. The other two shipping clerks were newer employees. Teamwork and mentoring were lacking. Approvals and sign-offs took a long time, resulting in delays.

There were errors in the communication from the office to the shipping room, errors in loading, and errors in the shipping paperwork. Sometimes items were not loaded in the proper order to facilitate easy unloading at destination or the optimum use of truck space. Often loaded product needed to be unloaded, then rearranged inside the truck, or trucks left not fully loaded. There were, on average, three errors per truckload. Whenever there was an error on the truck (too many or not enough of an item), customers would become irate because they did not get what they ordered or their item was shipped to a different customer.

The Kaizen Agenda

Since the current state was found to be eight hours to load one truck, and since not all activities were visual, the team decided to videotape only the steps where there were actual movements of the shipping room employees or of products. A full, detailed process flow diagram was created for the team to study value-added versus non-value-added activities, the SIPOC linkage, and handoffs of both information and product. Several spaghetti diagrams were drawn to help understand and analyze non-value-added motion and transportation wastes. Internal steps (tasks that could be accomplished only when the truck is physically at the dock) and external steps (tasks that could be done before the arrival or departure of the truck or in parallel while the truck was waiting at the dock) and the times taken were tabulated. Some available benchmarks were used to set the improvement goals. The five whys and fishbone diagram were useful tools in root cause analysis and Pareto charts for ranking improvement ideas. Project management was also discussed, especially the use of Gantt charts.

The team created an agenda, which included:

- Kaizen team formation, training, data collection, and analysis

- Creation, review, and analysis of the process flow diagram

- Study of the video (previously filmed) to separate individual tasks, internal and external time, non-value-added tasks/time, and so forth

- Creation of the spaghetti diagrams

- Root cause analyses of various issues identified

- Ranking of improvement opportunities according to importance

- Brainstorming and consensus building for the future state improvement plan with quantifiable goals

- Implementation of the agreed-upon plan (as a pilot run)

- Monitor results

- Create the 30-day action item list to tie up all loose ends

- Put together a plan for creating lean standard work with a training plan, necessary logs, and checklists, so as to capture the gains

- Presentation to key employees and management

The facilitator had the team identify all the different wastes present in the current state. The members were able to pinpoint all eight wastes to varying degrees. Next the facilitator helped the team identify which lean building blocks would be most appropriate to attack each of the wastes. The team, after brainstorming, came up with:

- Streamlined layout

- 5S

- Visual controls

- POUS

- Standard work (after time observation and work combination studies)

- Quality at the source

- Continuous improvement

The team decided that, while all these lean techniques would be useful to implement to reach a consistently improved future state, it would be impossible to implement all of them in the three days of the kaizen event. The team agreed to place them on the 30-day action item list with a Gantt chart to monitor progress and to make sure that all improvement tasks would be completed on time. The team set a future state goal of reducing average loading time from the current eight hours to four hours, with *no* errors.

Kaizen Results

The team simulated one pilot run and found that it could actually load a truck properly in approximately one hour with no errors. This was 87 percent improvement (though the goal in this case was originally only 50 percent). The accountant in the kaizen team calculated the annual savings to be $702,624 (with the cost of the project at $32,820). Other benefits included better teamwork and simplified training for new employees.

STANDARD WORK IN CUSTOMER SERVICE

Background

From a previous kaizen event, a team determined that the customer service department would benefit from establishing standard work for the order entry process. The team already had detailed ISO 9001:2000 procedures, but two things stood out: (1) the procedures weren't always followed, and (2) there were no time elements associated with the tasks.

A good cross-functional team was put together for this event. Some of the team members had participated in the earlier kaizen event that had identified this event, and others had some lean training before. The team consisted of: a customer service manager, three customer service representatives including a trainer, the lean champion, a Six Sigma Black Belt, a representative from sales, a scheduler, a continuous improvement engineer, and a facilitator.

The team determined its expectations as follows:

- Streamline order processing flow

- Use a team approach to creating standard work

- Have as much standard work as possible

- Have a baseline set for customer service

- Make training easier

- Consolidate and streamline processes

- Find ways to cut time anywhere

- Make order entry simple and easy

Current State

Team members received a half day of training on standard work that included the types of forms used in standard work such as the standard work sheet, standard work combination sheet, time observation form, spaghetti diagrams, and one-point lessons. During the training they learned when and why they should use standard work. They also participated in a class exercise where they had to record time observations on the facilitator performing a task, create a standard work combination sheet, a standard work sheet, and a one-point lesson. In the afternoon they took a simple process in the customer service area and created the same forms. The following day they determined which processes were the most important for them to study and they split into teams to create the standard work. They used the process outlined in Figure 6.22.

The method that worked well for this team was to break into subteams of three people each. One concentrated on watching the process and determining when steps were completed, another operated the stopwatch, while the third person observed. Each subteam had at least one person from customer service who knew the process.

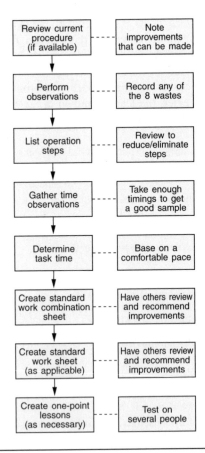

Figure 6.22   Standard work process flow diagram.

The first step was for the groups to review the procedure (if one existed). This allowed them time to get a feel for the process and also to mark any inconsistencies or changes. The next step was to just observe the customer service representatives (CSRs) perform the task. This once again, gave them a comfort level with the task. After the observations, the team wrote down the steps as they should be done. This in itself was an eye-opener. One of the questions that came up was, "If we already knew that there was a better way, should we just write it down that way?" The team members decided that they would write it down as it was currently being performed with no changes, this way they would have the true current state situation and baseline times. The team then performed many time observations, trying to observe several people performing the task. See Figure 6.23. Team members even thought it would be fun to time themselves; they wanted to see where they fit into the mix. On a side note, later we found out that there was a little fun, gentle ribbing from one CSR to the next on their

Date		Observer			Location							
Cyclic												
ID	Operation	1	2	3	4	5	6	7	8	9	10	Task time	Comments
1													
2													
3													
4													
5													
6													
7													
8													
9													
10													
Total													
Noncyclic													
1													
2													
3													
Total													

Figure 6.23 Time observation form.

times. The team fully understood that people were going to act differently just because they were watching the process, due to the Hawthorne effect.

After they collected enough times to satisfy themselves that they had a good representation of the process, team members determined the task time for the process steps. The task time was not necessarily the average of the times. The team took into consideration the experience level of the CSR, the range of times, and being able to perform the task comfortably for an eight-hour day.

Once armed with the task times, the team created the standard work combination sheet, a standard work sheet (if it was needed), and some one-point lessons to better explain some of the process steps. See Figure 6.24.

The team immediately found better, faster, and easier ways to complete these tasks. The CSRs were a wealth of input for improvements. For instance, the teams observed that even though they were trained by the same person, CSRs still performed the steps slightly differently. Sometimes this was good and sometimes this was bad. For example, one CSR took 12 minutes to perform a task that another CSR took only eight minutes to complete. The CSR who took longer was checking and rechecking things that didn't need to be rechecked (overprocessing waste). Another major breakthrough occurred when the team discovered little tricks of the trade that all the CSRs developed over time. Things like how to enter information only once (versus several times), using hot keys, and using copy and paste or other shortcuts built into the order entry system. This way the team built the best of the best into the new standard work.

Implementation

As part of the actual implementation phase to roll this out across the entire customer service department, the team took some time to determine why there may be some resistance to people following standard work. Team members brainstormed ideas of what people would say about standard work or not using or following standard work. Table 6.7 shows the result.

Results and Lessons Learned

The team realized that it wasn't finished when the kaizen event ended. It created a 30-day action item list and calendar that included the following tasks:

- Decide where to display the standard work

- Create more standard work

- Train people on the new standard work

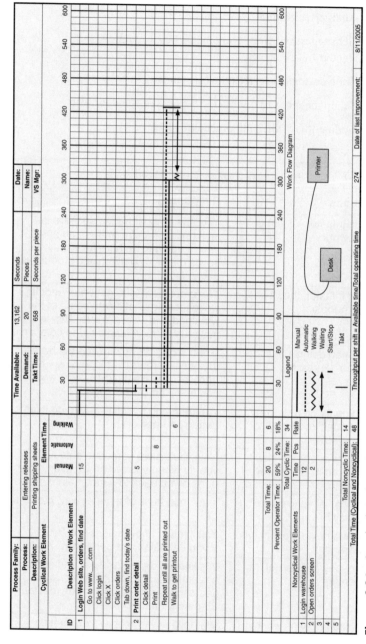

Figure 6.24 Standard work combination sheet—before.

- Audit after training

- Get suggestions from everyone on how to improve the standard work

- Train customer service on what standard work is

- Set up meetings to discuss the benefits of standard work

- Update ISO 9001:2000 procedures

Table 6.7 Reasons for resistance to standard work.

Objections	Responses
1. If I do it faster, I'll just get more work.	You'll be doing it better, so there is less rework. You're more of an asset. You're going to be here for eight hours, so we might as well make it productive and easier.
2. If I do it faster, they'll get rid of people.	We're not looking to get rid of people; we're looking to alleviate some of the workload and stress levels. This will make us more valuable to the company.
3. I've been doing it this way for 15 years.	Great! You'll be able to see the benefits that we all created. Things have changed from the way we did it 15 years ago. You *can* teach an old dog new tricks.
4. Are you trying to tell me that I don't know how to do my job?	We are trying to find a way to do it faster, better, and easier.
5. If I show everyone else how to do it, I'll lose my importance (or job security).	Now you'll have someone able to back you up when you are on vacation, so you don't come back to a mountain of work.
6. Why do I have to do it this way?	If you can think of a better way, prove it.
7. This will never work in our department.	You'll never know unless you try. If you can think of a better way, prove it.
8. Every day is different, "it depends . . . "	We know it depends; we are trying to streamline 65 percent of your day so you can react to the other unexpected 35 percent much easier.
9. This stuff doesn't work. This is another flavor of the month. We've already done this before.	We have saved money from these types of events and it will pay off in our profit sharing.

Besides creating standard work for tasks, some of the quick victories included actually shaving time off current processes. One process went from four minutes to two minutes each time CSRs performed the task, which could be several (even hundreds) times a day. See Figure 6.25. By using the spaghetti diagrams, the team discovered that it would be beneficial to move some of the items in the office, such as the copier and printers. This also made it extremely easy to train new CSRs. The training time went from hours for a particular task to minutes.

The team captured its lessons learned from the event:

- Don't bite off more than you can chew.

- Small projects can turn into large projects fast (the Godzilla factor).

- Use cross-functional teams, it gives an outsider's perspective.

- Make the graph on the standard work combination sheet larger.

- Determine what the content of the standard work sheet is for.

- People doing tasks on a daily basis do them so fast they don't even think about them.

- Create a very detailed standard work sheet for training level and one for functional level.

- It can take a lot of time and effort to create your first standard work sheets.

- Even simple things can be pretty involved (many steps).

- There can still be a lot of variation within a single step.

- There was some friendly competition between CSRs to do it faster.

- Even though people are doing the same task, they do it differently.

- We need to know Word or Excel better.

- It will take you longer than you think in the beginning.

- Make sure people don't bother you when you are getting this done.

- You'll do a whole lot of walking and watching the process.

- The first time you do it is not the last time you do it. Keep updating and improving the standard work.

- Be aware that some steps are very fast and need to be observed more than once.

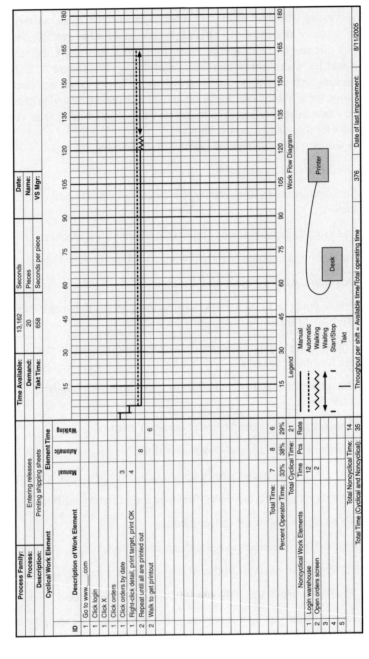

Figure 6.25 Standard work combination sheet—after.

A TOTAL PRODUCTIVE MAINTENANCE EVENT

Background

This TPM event was performed at a forging company that was extremely reliant on its equipment. Any downtime on key equipment could cause late deliveries or bumping in the schedule. On certain equipment, if the right spare parts weren't on hand, it could take weeks, even months, to get them. Also, the union operators were paid on a pay-for-performance scale that meant equipment downtime would reduce their pay rate.

The company's TPM design team wanted to go through a kaizen event so it could experience one before it started to schedule other events. This was its mock event to learn more about how to perform a TPM kaizen event and to better prepare teams in the future.

There were many pieces of equipment that the team considered to kick off its kaizen experience. The team had narrowed it down to two pieces of equipment; both were critical to its operations. One was a press and the other was a heavy-duty conveyor. After a discussion with the team and realizing the time constraint of only three days to perform the improvements, the team chose the conveyor. You might think that a conveyor is just part of transportation waste, but in this case it was used to cool the forgings while moving them to the next operation (which is value-added). This wasn't your run-of-the-mill conveyor. The company designed and built these conveyors. It was a heavy-duty design to be able to withstand the punishing environment that it was used in.

The TPM design team included: a production supervisor, a storeroom supervisor, a continuous improvement coordinator, a pressman, a millwright, a maintenance supervisor, a metallurgist, and an outside facilitator. The design team had been in existence for about eight months so team members were used to working together. The design team had also been part of other kaizen events such as 5S or QCO and also had been through training in lean and TPM.

Current State

The team prepared ahead of time and thought it would be a good idea to use a high-pressure sprayer, wash the conveyor, and then paint it before the event. The facilitator recommended that next time the team leave the equipment in whatever state it is currently in, so that everyone could see what it normally looks like. Also, cleaning and painting it conceals any leaks, drips, and buildup.

One of the key features of performing this type of event involves getting to the root cause of the breakdowns. The team took adequate time in identifying the breakdowns and their actual causes. This helped team members before they got to the brainstorming stage because they came up with ideas on how to fix problem areas and avoid breakdowns or lost time in the future. They utilized a breakdown analysis worksheet and used the five whys technique to assist in correcting the major issues. See Figure 6.26.

Part of the discussion included what was dubbed the Godzilla factor. The Godzilla factor is described like this: when Godzilla was a baby he was cute, some say even cuddly, but then he grows and grows until he destroys entire cities! The moral of the story is to take care of the little problems before they become big problems. The team came up with 13 reasons why little problems become big problems:

1. We don't know the equipment [well] enough

2. We don't look for the little things

3. The equipment is able to run, so don't bother with it

4. Just keep it running for now

5. Run it until it breaks

6. We don't have the time to check the little things

7. That's not my job

8. Take care of it on third shift

9. Leave it for the next person

10. We have bigger problems elsewhere to take care of

11. This is the least of my problems right now

12. We don't have the people right now; they're working on something else

13. We don't have the parts to fix it anyway

Another issue discovered was that even though the company builds about four new conveyors a year, there was no bill of materials (BOM) available and the drawing was not up to date. A millwright mentioned that when told to build a conveyor, workers look at the blueprint and see what materials they have on hand and order the rest. This obviously caused many of the conveyors to be slightly different in design.

Breakdown Analysis Worksheet

Machine/equipment		Area		
Date of occurrence		Time		
Downtime from		Downtime to	Total	
Issue				
Why?		Man		
Why?		Machine		
Why?		Material		
Why?		Method		
Why?		Measurement		
Root cause		Drawing		
Interim solution		Approved by		
Time to repair		Performed by		
Cost				

Permanent solution		Approved by	
Time to repair		Performed by	
Cost			
Closeout			
Checklist created?	[ ] Yes	[ ] No, explain	
One-point lesson created?	[ ] Yes	[ ] No, explain	
Include in autonomous maintenance?	[ ] Yes	[ ] No, explain	
All appropriate personnel trained	[ ] Yes	[ ] No, explain	
Lessons learned			

Figure 6.26   Breakdown analysis worksheet.

While developing its vision, the team created nine categories and determined 35 goals for the project:

Safety

1. Stop/start/reverse buttons

2. All guards functional and in place

3. Wiring not frayed, not burnt, waterproofed

4. Design a way to trap the scale

Quality

5. Prevent hot nicks

6. Prevent forging jam-ups

7. Correct speed of conveyor

Ease of maintenance

8. Quick disconnects on electrical

9. Standardize sprockets, chain, gear box, motor, wheels/castors

10. Easy to lube

11. Easy to roll/move

12. Make it easier to adjust belt

13. Label the conveyor number, all lube points, lube type, adjusters

14. Update the blueprints

15. Review the current preventive maintenance (PM) and modify

16. Mount starters on the stationary presses

5S

17. Clean and inspect and lube schedule

18. Contain scale

19. Visuals—arrows, labels, directions

20. Color code safety guards, lube lines, electrical

Unplanned downtime

21. Improve PM schedule

22. Daily checklists

23. Better equipment history log/information

24. Find a better way to monitor wear

25. Eliminate broken wheels

Planned downtime

26. Follow PM schedule

27. Determine ways to do PMs faster

28. Coordinate 5S with PMs

Changeover

29. Easier way to adjust plate

30. Make it lighter, easier to move

Minor stops

31. Eliminate adjustments of belts

32. Eliminate jam-ups

Other

33. Slow cool conveyors at correct speed

34. No wheels—can't push them anyway

35. All conveyors are standardized (except length of conveyors)

The Kaizen Event

The team used the sticky-note method of brainstorming and came up with 12 categories and 60 viable improvements for the conveyor! These ideas were placed on the 30-day action item list. As part of the 30-day action item list, the team used the effort and impact model. By rating the effort and impact by low, medium, and high, the team was able to choose the most important ideas to work on first (low effort and high impact).

Results and Lessons Learned

The team wanted to capture and share some of the good ideas that it had implemented and recognize the people who helped make it happen. A quick

---

One Good Idea

Problem: Not fast and easy to make adjustments to the belt or to know when the belt has stretched too much.

Solution: Place a scale on each side with a yellow mark to help make alignments faster.

Before	After
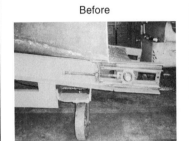	

Benefits: Reduces the amount of time to make adjustments and now able to track belt wear/stretch.

Thanks to: Tom, John, Jeff

Figure 6.27   "One good idea" sheet.

and easy tool for this is a "one good idea" sheet. This is a simple 8½" × 11" form that captures the nature of the problem, the solution, before and after photos, benefits, and appreciation for those who made it happen. See Figure 6.27 for an example.

As part of standardization, the team created PM schedules, autonomous maintenance (AM) schedules, and one-point lessons for cleaning, inspecting, and lubricating the conveyor. Besides completing its 30-day action item list, the team had a discussion about how to sustain the gains it had created. In the near term it decided to use the AM schedule and audit it, have the project leader audit the AM schedule for 30 days and then transfer that responsibility to the crew, and, in 20 days, perform the PMs as a team to see how everything is going.

To make sure that future events ran smoothly and to continually improve its efforts, the team captured 23 lessons learned. The list is:

1. Don't worry about what can't be done; focus on what we can do.

2. Don't bite off more than you can chew.

3. Not everybody will be satisfied, especially if their idea wasn't implemented.

4. Be prepared that many things may change as more input is gathered.

5. Have the right number of millwrights and electricians on the team.

6. Prioritize the ideas with A, B, C, impact and effort, 30-day and "never."

7. Need a high level of cooperation from other departments and management to be able to close out the 30-day list.

8. The root cause analysis/breakdown analysis was important to the brainstorming efforts.

9. Make sure people are thinking about the six big losses of TPM during brainstorming.

10. Keep an eye on scope creep.

11. Have a trainer per unit in the cell and a facilitator for the training portion.

12. If it has a low effort and a high impact and makes the crew happier or the job easier, we should try to do it.

13. TPM is *not* just to clean and fix things; find the root cause of the problem.

14. Plan and prepare better for materials needed for an event.

15. As we do more of the same types of equipment, we will know better what to have.

16. Need to be more prepared with documentation (PM systems, blueprints, check sheets).

17. We definitely need more millwright help.

18. Have a facilitator to record information on the computer and the trainer at the piece of equipment

19. Dedicate people from the beginning to the end and rotate people. People have to gel, it takes a team.

20. A TPM kaizen event on a press will take more than three days.

21. Once standards are created it is easier to modify them as needed.

22. Teams should be made of volunteers versus assigned.

23. The project leader has to keep people on track and make sure they are working together.

By using this event the team members learned how to perform a TPM event and learned many valuable lessons to improve their implementation methods. After this event they created a schedule to continue on their work to include other equipment and participants.

VALUE STREAM MAPPING—FROM RFQ TO DELIVERY

Background

The company specializes in custom orders for its products and has decades of experience. Originally this organization wanted to perform a value stream mapping event on its RFQ process only. Through a conversation with the vice president, the authors quickly discovered that the company had not performed any higher-level or big-picture maps. The authors suggested that the company start there first, so it could see the entire process before trying to drill down in a specific area because trying to perform a process-level map first may create problems by optimizing one area and suboptimizing another. By including RFQ along with the rest of the processes, the team was able to have a complete VSM.

Through experience, the method that the authors use for a VSM kaizen event typically takes three days. Prior to the event the authors meet with the value stream manager or other top executives to explain the process, help determine the scope, and the team members. The team should be made up of about seven cross-functional managers or supervisors. These people need to be able to see the whole picture and the potential for improvement. This team included: the vice president of operations (who had been with the company for only six months at this point), a design engineer, a sales and area business manager, a process engineering coordinator, the manufacturing team leader, a customer service account manager, a manufacturing planner/buyer, the information services manager, and a facilitator. This was a good cross-functional team that represented many aspects of the organization.

The scope of a VSM kaizen project is extremely important. Many organizations are too narrowly focused in their scope or try to bite off more than they can chew. Stick to a process family to see the entire picture first before drilling down to specific aspects of your value stream. The four-step process for value stream mapping is:

1. Determine the process family

2. Draw the current state map

3. Create a future state map

4. Develop the action plan to get to the improved future state

Current State

First the team determined the process family by going through the different process steps in the organization. It decided to concentrate on an RFQ–new design product family. The team discovered 21 high-level processing steps. To create the current state map, shown in Figure 6.28, the team walked the flow from the first contact with the customer through quoting, ordering materials, production, and shipping. Team members interviewed the people performing the tasks to collect data for the map. During this phase there was a lot of discovery, including people from the production floor learning what actually occurs in the office and vice versa. Also, the managers and supervisors on the team were able to hear how their people performed their

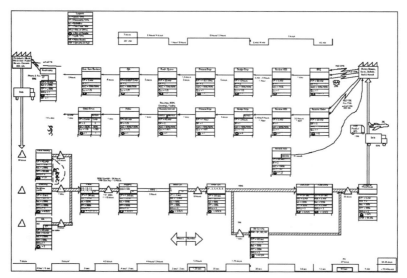

Figure 6.28 Current state map.

tasks and learned what made their jobs more difficult. During the walk-through the team also noted many of the eight wastes of lean.

Future State

To create the future state, the team reviewed basic lean principles such as QCO, flow or cellular manufacturing, and 5S. Team members went through a list of prepared questions to help them create the future state. The team was very open about what needed improvement: processing forms, waiting and queue time in the office functions, and specific manufacturing techniques. See Figure 6.29. The original lead time (the time when the order is taken to the time it is shipped) was over 60 days, which did not include the time waiting for the customer to reply to the RFQ.

Results

A major improvement included creating an office cell for the quoting process. As discovered in the current state, the quote had to pass through

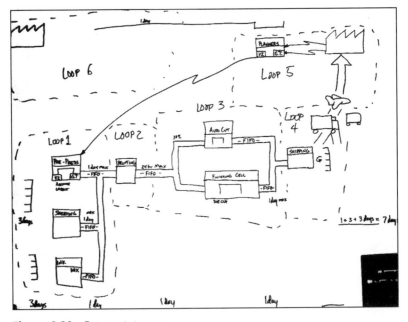

Figure 6.29 Future state map.

Table 6.8   Before and after times for RFQs.

	Initial quoting process	Quote review	Raw material ordering and receiving	Manufacturing
Before	20 days	20 days	5 days	21 days
After	5 days	1 day	5 days	3 days

several stages and departments. This initial quoting process took about 20 days. In the future state, by having a team work together to create the quote, that time went down to an average of five days. See Table 6.8. The overall lead time went from about 66 days to about 14 days!

Two other important outcomes resulted from this event. First of all, the new vice president commented that he learned more about the company during this event than he did in the prior six months. This was an eye-opening experience. It proves the point that new management employees should participate in a value stream mapping event soon after joining the organization for two reasons: (1) they can provide the outsider's point-of-view and are able to question everything, and (2) they can learn more about the entire flow within the company (or lack thereof).

The other important outcome was that the team learned that most support functions or office functions do not believe that lean can apply to them. This company was able to create an office cell to improve the time it takes to generate a quote. An additional side benefit was that people started working as a team by performing their tasks together.

VISUAL WORKPLACE

Background

This example is actually an amalgamation of several kaizen events where visual controls are the main focus. It is very common to combine visual controls with other aspects of lean such as 5S or QCO. But visual controls are so powerful on their own that they deserve special attention. A typical visual kaizen event can be performed in about two days. On the first day there is training on visual controls and then the rest of the time is spent implementing the visual improvements. A quick and easy training exercise to show the value of visual controls is presented in Sidebar 6.3.

Hide and Seek or How Can Visual Controls Help Me?
Class Exercise

OVERVIEW

This exercise will give the participants a hands-on demonstration on how a visual system can make locating an item quick, efficient, and simple. This exercise will demonstrate the following concepts:

- Importance of visual systems

- Communication and information flow

- Value-added versus non-value-added activities

- Waste (muda)

- Teamwork

- Brainstorming

SUPPLIES

- Small items (for example, your corporate logo coffee mug, pen, key chain, or knick-knack) to be found. The number of items is based on the number of teams (four to eight people per team).

- Sticky notes, paper, and different color markers to make signs.

- Flip chart and markers to make signs or record comments *(optional)*.

- Masking tape to post signs.

- 3" × 5" index cards or similar, folded in half with the item that the "new employee" will look for (see small items list).

- A stopwatch for each team.

Continued

Continued

AGENDA

Typically the exercise can be run in 15 to 30 minutes. Adjust the agenda accordingly.

	Approximate time
Introduction and team assignments	5 minutes
Round 1	5 minutes
Opportunities for improvements	10 minutes
Round 2	1 minute
Review	5 minutes
	Total: 26 minutes

STEPS

Introduction and Team Assignments

- Divide the group into teams of approximately four to eight people per team.

- Get one (1) volunteer per team to be the "new employee." His or her role is to go get a critical part because a machine has broken down and it is imperative that they get it up and running again immediately!

- Get one (1) volunteer per team to be the "timer" and give that person a stopwatch.

- Have the "new employee" leave the room (so he or she cannot see or hear what is going on in the room) until the facilitator calls that person back in.

  - Once out of the room, let the new employee randomly pick an index card with the item that he or she will be looking for.

  - Note which new employee (and team) has which item.

  - Instruct the new employee that he or she is not allowed to communicate with the teams in any way.

Continued

- Give each team the item that their new employee will be looking for.

- Have the teams put them in an inconspicuous (not easily seen) place, such as behind items on a table, under a table, in a corner, etc. Make sure that it is not easy to find right away, nor too difficult.

- Instruct the teams that they are not allowed to communicate with the new employee (for example, speaking, motioning, winking, coughing, and so on), except to say "hurry up!" or "we need that part right now!"

- Have the timer ready to start timing how long its takes the new employee to find the item as soon as they walk in the room.

Round 1

- Bring the new employee back into the room to find the item.

- Have the timer see how long its takes to find the item and record the time.

Opportunities for Improvement

- Once again, have the new employees leave the room. Explain that they get a little break for volunteering, but make sure not to leave the area.

- Have the team brainstorm and develop visual signals to make it easier for the new employee to find the item. Have the teams make signs, arrows, and so on, to help their new employee. Remind them to think from the new employee's point of view. Can the signs be easily seen? Are they placed in appropriate spots? Do they make sense?

- Have the team put the item in an inconspicuous place and not the same place as before. Make sure that it is *not* easy to find right away.

Continued

- Have the timer ready to start timing how long its takes the new employee to find this item.

Round 2

- Bring the new employee back into the room to search for the item.

- Remember, the team is not allowed to help the new employee. They can only tell him or her to hurry up or go faster.

- Have the timer record the time.

Review

- Review the times and talk about what worked, what didn't, and whether they have eliminated waste and non-value added activities (search time, motion waste, waiting waste, and so on).

- Let the new employee explain how he or she felt in the first round as compared to the second round. This will help explain the "soft side" or human side of lean.

As a reward for volunteering, allow each new employee volunteer to keep the item.

The following is a list of examples of visual controls with corresponding photos:

1. *Lean communication board.* This is an example of a communication center that can be set up to provide employees information related to a company's lean efforts. See Figure 6.30.

2. *Access panel.* Anyone can see through the metal screen to ensure proper operation and for preventive maintenance. See Figure 6.31.

3. *Color coded bottles.* Color coding makes it easy to see from a distance; translucent bottles make it easy to see the level of liquid inside. Remember to back up color coding with words for those who are color-blind. See Figure 6.32.

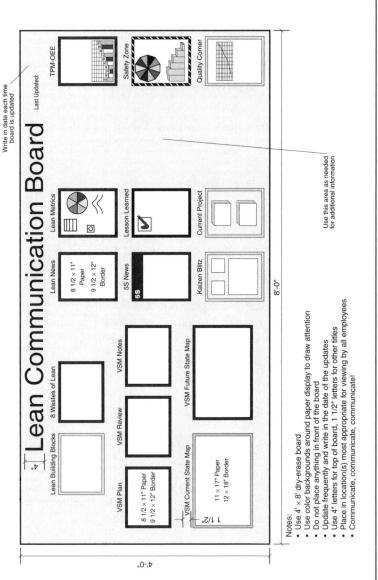

Figure 6.30   A sample communication center.

Figure 6.31   An example of an access panel.

Figure 6.32   An example of unorganized bottles on the left and translucent, color coded bottles on the right.

4. *Lines on floor.* Make it easier to see where items belong (or don't belong). Diagonal striped lines on the floor mean no parking. See Figure 6.33.

5. *Stripes on stairs.* To improve safety, mark the edge of stairs with yellow paint. See Figure 6.34.

6. *Alignment line.* A simple line can save minutes (or even hours) during repairs and maintenance or even to ensure proper operation. See Figure 6.35.

7. *Labeling stations.* Use large numbers or letters to identify stations on equipment. See Figure 6.36.

8. *Control panel.* Make the control panel easy to see from a distance; this improves operation and safety. See Figure 6.37.

9. *Gages.* Mark gages to show the proper range. See Figure 6.38.

Figure 6.33 In the photo on the left, there are no visual lines on the floor, while in the photo on the right, the areas are clearly marked.

Figure 6.34 The two photos show the same set of stairs, but safety stripes have been added to the set on the right.

Figure 6.35 The white line on the center gear shows alignment at a glance.

Figure 6.36 The large number on the machine on the right identifies the workstation.

Figure 6.37 The control panel on the right is clearly marked to see from a distance.

Figure 6.38 The acceptable range on the gage is clearly marked.

10. *Safety lines on floor.* Reduce chances for a safety incident by brightly painted potential hazards. See Figure 6.39.

11. *Fluid level.* Mark the proper level of oil to prevent problems or breakdowns. See Figure 6.40.

12. *Parts racks.* Organize parts racks and label what goes where. See Figure 6.41.

13. *Label office equipment.* Clearly label with information such as who to contact when there is a problem, where replenishment supplies are kept, and so forth. See Figure 6.42.

14. *Range lines for doors.* Simple dashed lines let people know how far a door opens to help prevent any injuries and enhance safety. See Figure 6.43.

15. *Shop work area.* Mark and label areas for work flow. See Figure 6.44.

Figure 6.39   Visual indicator of possible safety hazard.

Figure 6.40   Lubricating oil visual level indicator.

Figure 6.41 Organized and clearly labeled shelves.

Figure 6.42 The fax machine is clearly labeled in case the user needs help.

Figure 6.43 Dashed lines on floor show how far gate swings open.

Figure 6.44 The lines on the floor show work areas and flow.

Visual Workplace Checklist

Through many years of experience the authors have created this list of items that should be considered when creating a visual workplace. This is meant to be a guide, provide insights, and give practical ideas of how and where visual controls can be utilized.

General

- Signs
- Lines
- Labels
- Color coding
- Charts, pictures, lights, scoreboards
- Company-specific symbols that are standardized
- Logs, lists
- Productivity goals
- Quality goals
- Delivery schedules
- Setup specification/standards
- Safety initiatives
- Attendance goals

- Team objectives
- Shadow boards
- Takt awareness
- Work standards
- Team goals versus performance
- Pictorial procedures (for example, ISO 9001:2000)
- Andon devices
- VSM current and future state maps
- Standard work instructions
- Tags
- Forms
- Training hours
- Employees' suggestions
- Cross-trained skills
- Employee awards
- Absenteeism
- Critical maintenance points
- Customer satisfaction goals
- Performance targets
- Performance visuals
- Delivery performance
- Stock turn
- Lead time
- Value-adding time
- Production costs (labor, material, and so on)
- Quality measures (first-pass yield, quality costs)
- Percent achieved to goals

- Productivity measures
- Accident hours
- Performance of equipment

Kanbans

- Production kanbans
- Withdrawal kanbans
- Supplier kanbans
- Empty marked space
- Two-bin system
- FIFO lanes
- Vendor-managed inventory
- Supermarket order-point and order-quantity

Maintenance

- Critical maintenance points
- Autonomous maintenance
- Clean
- Inspection points
- Change oil
- Change filter
- Grease
- Uptime goal versus actual, and trends
- Overall equipment effectiveness (OEE)

7 + 1 quality tools and techniques

- Pareto charts
- Fishbone diagram
- Histograms
- Control charts
- Run charts

- Check sheets
- Scatter diagram
- Flowcharts

Management and Planning Tools

- Matrices, diagrams, graphs, and charts

Visual Management in 5M

- Manpower (Operators)
  - Worker morale–related
  - Suggestions made
  - Suggestions acted on
  - Employee recognition
  - Accidents
  - Skill-related
  - Training done
  - Training planned
  - Cross-training
  - Standards related
  - One-point lessons
  - Displays of acceptable versus rejectable
- Machines
  - Lubrication levels
  - Transparent covers so as to make the inside visible
  - Temperature, pressure gages
  - Feed, speed, and revolutions per minute
  - Machine performance (throughput)
- Materials
  - Inventory levels
  - Color coding of different grades, parts, components, and so on

- Material address (location)
- Part number, heat number, and so on
- Methods
  - Standard work sheets
  - Sequence of work
  - Processing cycle time
  - Safety issues
  - Quality checkpoints
  - Tools needed
  - What to do when variability happens
- Measurements
  - Safe operating ranges
  - Improvement measures and trends
  - Calibration records/labels
  - Daily production targets and actuals

7

Cost–Benefit Analysis for Kaizen Projects

Just as in Six Sigma projects, it is important to calculate and communicate the cost savings derived from kaizen events. If the benefits do not exceed the costs involved in doing the kaizen, obviously the project is not worthwhile. North American managers are famous for focusing on only the financial results of a Kaizen or process improvement project and not the other benefits achieved. The payback period is a simple, yet common metric that is used in deciding if an event should be done or not. Net present value (NPV), return on investment (ROI), discounted cash flow, and internal rate of return (IRR) are other, more complex calculations. These methods all have their strengths. But if those are the only metrics used to pick projects, then we may be missing other important and innovative improvements.

In many situations, there might be more than one kaizen with net positive dollar benefit. In such cases it helps the kaizen teams and management to prioritize which project to work on first, through the comparison of the cost–benefit expected from each. Invariably we have been able to determine a monetary benefit of the project, but it is usually the other gains that make the biggest impact. Kaizen events not only help reduce costs, but they can also help the top line—sales and revenues. By improving quality, on-time delivery, or service levels, customers would be more likely to buy from our firm than the competition. So by affecting the top line and costs we are automatically improving the bottom line or profits.

In many kaizens, there are tangible dollar benefits plus various intangible advantages as well. The latter might include improvements in safety, quality, ergonomics, search time, morale, customer satisfaction, teamwork, and employee retention, just to name a few. An experienced lean champion or value stream manager also would be able to quantify these intangibles in dollar terms—but not always. If this is possible, we are able to compare apples to apples. The cost side is more easily calculated: labor and materials plus any expenses involving external consultant or facilitator, if used. Lean kaizen team members pulled away from daily work for the duration of these events constitute the labor costs. Enlist the help of the accounting department to calculate financial results. In our experience the company's accountants have been more than happy to help with this part of the project. See Sidebar 7.1.

The example in Table 7.1 is just an illustration of a SMED kaizen for setup time reduction; this sample shows how cost–benefit in such cases can be calculated. Readers can use it as a template and customize it to their own specific situation. One of the major benefits of a setup time reduction kaizen is the expected result in lowered inventory requirements. Cost accountants say that the total inventory carrying costs could be as high as 30 percent of the inventoried material cost.

Sidebar 7.1

Accountant Saves the Day

In a particular QCO kaizen event, the company had to change the target area the day before the event due to unforeseen circumstances. This clearly led to confusion for the participants. With the help of an experienced facilitator and a willing team, they were still able to make many improvements.

The original changeover time before the event for this particular piece of equipment was 20 minutes. After applying the SMED technique, the team was able to reduce it to 10 minutes. Because of the nature of this process and equipment, there was a definite improvement in teamwork, standardization, reduced motion waste, and so on, but there was a general concern from management that it wouldn't have much of a financial impact. By using a corporate accountant who had participated in other kaizen events, the team showed a $20,000 annual savings (even after all the costs and expenses). When the facilitator realized that there was such a small financial improvement (the lowest he had ever achieved in a kaizen event), he expressed dismay to the accountant that he was sorry they couldn't deliver more of a financial benefit.

The accountant replied with a statement that lifted the spirits of everyone on the team when he exclaimed, "I'll take this kind of improvement any day. You have helped the company financially, but more importantly, you have helped us improve our process."

Table 7.1 SMED cost–benefit example.

ID	Item	Per Setup Before	Per Setup After	Expense	Savings	One-time only	Recurring
1	Setup time	4 hrs.	30 mins.				
2	Equipment time value	$100	$100				
3	Variable cost for running equipment—utilities, overhead, and so on	$50/hr.	$50/hr.				
4	Number of setups per day—assume lot sizes are cut in half after project	1	2				
5	Number of working days per year	240	240				
6	Cost for employee training time	$0	$500				
7	Scrap due to first-piece inspection and adjustments	$150	$50				
8	Dedicated tool cart expenses	$0	$1,000				
9	New tools, equipment, gages, and so on	$0	$5,000				
10	Setup person wages and benefits	$25/hr.	$25/hr.				
11	Annual carrying cost of inventory	$250,000	$125,000				
12	Cost savings due to newly freed-up space, quality, and so on	$0	$20,000				
13	Cost avoidance—not having to buy another machine (amortized)	$0	$50,000				
14	Cost savings associated with less machine wear and tear, safety, ergonomics, and so on	$0	$15,000				
15	Benefits from better customer service, increased market penetration, and so on	$0	$50,000				
16	Facilitator cost for four-day event	$0	$8,000				
17	Internal employee time for four-day event	$0	$6,720				
18	Incidental costs during project—lunches, t-shirts, and so on	$0	$800				

Note: demand exceeds current capacity

Table 7.2 Sample 5S benefits worksheet.

Benefit	Improvement (%↑↓, $, time, and so on)
5S resources	
5S standards	
Attitude	
Better cleanliness	
Better communication	
Better flow	
Better orderliness	
Better organization	
Better production streamlining	
Better quality	
Breakage, unusable, damage, obsolete items	
Color coding	
Ease of obtaining information/ location	
Employee involvement	
Increased efficiency	
Increased safety	
Fewer breakdowns	
Less inventory	
Less search time	
Management support	
More ergonomic	
Pleasant place to work	
POUS	
Prevention of dirt, grime, and contamination	
Reward and recognition	
Sense of ownership	
Space saved	
Teamwork	
Useful and necessary inspections	
Visual controls	

Kaizen teams usually surprise themselves by achieving the aggressive stretch goals that they set for themselves during the planning stage. Similarly, the benefits derived also can be substantial.

The benefits captured from a 5S kaizen event are a mix of quantitative (numbers) and qualitative (feelings) measures, as Table 7.2 shows. A simple visual analysis tool for qualitative measures is arrow analysis. Just draw an arrow based on how the team feels about the improvement. If everything is going well, draw the arrow pointing straight up. If it is a failure, draw it straight down. An arrow drawn anywhere in between shows some level of progress or improvement.

Conclusion

In this book, the authors wanted to present to the reader, first, the basic concepts of lean and kaizen, then illustrate through examples how to perform their own kaizens on the shop floor, in the office, and in purely service environments. These examples are based on real-world lean kaizens, which, we hope, clarify and reinforce the theoretical concepts even further.

The reader should be able to benefit from the copious number of checklists, forms, and figures provided in the book during the planning stage of your own kaizen(s). Our suggestion would be to customize these to suit your specific project. Most of them were developed during the 200 or so lean engagements the authors have participated in.

What's next for the reader? From this point on, it is possible to create your own kaizens and start your lean journey by rereading and referring to the specific concepts and examples provided in the book. Also, we would like to provide some useful Web sites (by no means is this list comprehensive):

www.5SSupply.com

www.ame.org

www.asq.org

www.asq.org/le

www.lean.org

www.mep.nist.gov

www.productivityinc.com

www.sme.org

www.superfactory.com

Any useful comment or suggestion for improvement of this book will be most gratefully accepted.

Appendix A
Kaizen Event Workbook Example

T his example of a setup time reduction workbook can be used as a guideline for performing a QCO/SMED four-day kaizen event. Customize it to meet your requirements or needs.

Kaizen Event Workbook

Kaizen Event
for
XYZ Company

Setup Time Reduction
On Work Center ABC

KAIZEN EVENT INTRODUCTION

A kaizen event is a team activity done, in this example, in four days, where significant gains are achieved in changeover time. As companies look to improve their processes and reduce inventories, they have started to focus attention on the time taken for machine changeover (setup) between production runs. The power of this approach is to allow small-batch production by making changeovers faster and more frequent.

A kaizen event builds on all the improvements for a total big effect, substantially completed in the set time frame. It is a project where the end result lies in the analysis and improvements of the elements that make up the steps of the problem to be solved.

In this four-day project, team members learn how to use the kaizen method for analyzing changeover work. Its application will bring the benefits of improved flexibility, shorter lead time, reduced inventory, and quality enhancement to the company. The team's goal is: to understand the principles of setup time reduction, the reasons behind each of the process steps, and improving them to reduce changeover time. Changeover time is defined as the time between the last good piece off one run and the first good piece off the next run.

THE KAIZEN EVENT

The basic steps of a kaizen event follow:

1. Name the setup reduction project the company will focus on.

2. Have an improvement goal in mind. The bigger the goal the better, for example, reduce setup time by 75 percent. Also, identify any quality-related problems associated with this machine. For example, keep in mind OEE, which is a combination of machine availability, machine performance (versus rated throughput), and first-pass yield.

3. List the team members who will be actively involved in reducing setup time. It is important for the management to provide adequate support. The team consists of:

   • Six to 10 members. (An ideal team would have a smaller number of members; but to have as many XYZ Company employees as possible trained in kaizen event techniques, up to 10 people can participate).

- The process owner (sponsor with clout) is the team leader.

- Team members can be setup people—operators, quality/first-piece inspectors, maintenance representatives, material handlers, tool room staff, and so on).

- Supervisors and/or key staff should be included.

- An outsider could be included.

- An accountant could be included.

- A facilitator should be included.

4. Videotape the actual changeover. Make two videotapes, if possible. For purpose of analysis, choose the setup where as many of the variables as possible get changed. See guidelines for using video, page 139.

5. Observe videotape and record the details of the changeover as it is presently being done. See process observation form, page 137.

- List each element of the setup process on the observation form.

- Record the time taken to perform each element.

- Record (if necessary) other details or facts observed or recalled in relation to each element.

6. Use a layout of the machine area to draw a spaghetti diagram of the walking path taken by operators during the changeover. (The company should provide layout of area where the machine being studied is located.)

- Calculate the distance walked in feet based on layout scale.

- Calculate the time spent walking based on the observation form. See changeover summary chart, page 140.

7. Brainstorm and simulate improvements where possible. Confirm the improvement goal. Can we do better than the 75 percent setup time reduction that we had in mind? Simulation can mean rearranging the work area, moving equipment, and so on, during their course of work. The facilitator will help the team to brainstorm and to do the simulation.

Process Observation Form

Date:

Company:

Process/Operation:

Page:

Operational element	Elapsed time	Actual time	Internal time	External time	Notes	Code

Use code: S = Setup preparation   R = Remove/attach   A = Adjustment   O = Other

8. XYZ Company should prepare a briefing package for all team members, containing the following information as relevant:

   - Customer requirements that can affect the number of variables in the setup

   - Machine capacity and production rates for the machine being studied

   - Layout, staffing, and defect rates

   - Documented instructions

   - Number and types of machine setups occurring daily, weekly, monthly

   Please note that too much information can confuse team members, so select only the kind of information that has a direct bearing or influence on the project.

9. The XYZ Company should determine how identified process improvement results will be presented at the end of the fourth day of the project. Usually the accounting department calculates identified potential dollar savings. The team members present the kaizen event process and improvement to company personnel.

10. The XYZ Company should plan communications to the people in the facility and the immediate work area where the kaizen event team will operate. Let employees know that no layoffs will take place as a result of kaizen event activities.

11. Notify support departments to have time available for supporting the kaizen event team experimentation for testing results.

12. The XYZ Company should prepare for administrative details such as meeting space, flip charts, writing materials, stopwatches, two video players, two TVs, and lunch arrangements. The team will need wall space to tape flip chart materials for review.

13. XYZ Company may wish to recognize kaizen event team members by taking a photo of them for inclusion in an internal newsletter. Also consider presenting tokens of recognition such as gift certificates, tickets to events, t-shirts, and so forth.

GUIDELINES FOR USING VIDEO

1. Clearly explain to those involved in the changeover what is being recorded and why.

2. Before taping, get a general idea of the setup operation and the important elements.

3. Make two videotapes. One of the general area and one focused on the actual changeover or operator's tasks.

4. If an operator is leaving the machine to get parts, follow him or her with the video camera. This will be useful in drawing the spaghetti diagram.

5. Imprint the time (with minutes and seconds) and date of the recording using a video timer. This is important to help speed up the analysis phase of the project and will preclude the use of a stopwatch.

6. People get anxious when they are recorded and tend to speed up as a result of the recording (Hawthorne effect)! Therefore, it is important to let them know that they should work at their normal pace and the purpose of the videotape is to analyze the changeover steps involved for improvement and not for recording how fast or slow they work. It is useful to state here that no one will be penalized as a result of the videotape.

7. During the videotaping of very long setups, it would be helpful if the operator could narrate what he or she is doing. Do this only if this does not pose any problems in the normal flow of a typical setup. The narration can be short, for example, "adjusting slide," or "removing gear," or "tightening bolt." If this is not possible, capture these steps during the video viewing on the first or second day of the kaizen event.

Changeover Summary Chart

Category code	Internal mins.	External mins.	Total mins.	Improvement ideas
Setup preparation (S) • Selecting tools, dies • Transporting • Poor layout that causes extra walking				
Remove/ attach (R) • Unbolting • Positioning • Bolting				
Adjustment (A) • Standard setting • Dimensioning • Centering • Test processing • Inspection • Feed amount				
Other • Position oil ports • Pneumatics • Hydraulics • Electrical • Any other connection				
Total				

DOCUMENTING THE DETAILS OF A SETUP TIME REDUCTION PROJECT

Document the details of the current process. Include setup time, number of changeovers per week/day, current problems/bottlenecks, and so forth.

1. Name the process. What is the focus of the kaizen event? For example, list machine, process, a specific part number, and so on.

2. State the goal of the kaizen event in measurable terms.

3. List team members.

4. Identify internal time and external time.

Basic Team Principles

- Actively listen
- Be sensitive to others
- Participate
- Remember: all ideas are equal
- Be punctual

- Use all forms of communication such as verbal, sticky notes, and hand signals.

- No criticisms of other person(s); discuss ideas only (until agreement is reached)

Team Objectives

- Learn to use the kaizen and lean tools

- Understand and analyze the process steps

- Try some new ways to do setups to achieve project goals

Assign Job Responsibilities

- Expert to interpret the videotape for the others (if necessary)

- Time study person

- Mapmaker for drawing the spaghetti diagram

- Scribe to write down the operation element as it is being explained

Analysis Phase

5. Analyze what is being done in the process.

Question	Ask	Action
What is the purpose?	5 *whys*	Eliminate unnecessary activity
Is this activity necessary? Can it be eliminated?		
Where and *when* is this being done?	5 *whys*	Combine or change place
Why does the step have to be done at this time? Can it be done earlier or later?		
Who is doing this?	5 *whys*	Combine or change person
Why is this person doing it? *Who* should do it?		
How is this being done?	5 *whys*	Simplify or improve method (Error-proof—poka-yoke)
Why are we doing it this way? Is there an easier way to achieve the same end result? *How* can this be done better?		

6. Brainstorm for improvement ideas.

7. Convert internal time to external time wherever possible. Write down ideas for streamlining internal time to external time.

8. Identify type of adjustment. Eliminate tool positioning, change item only once, and minimize material variation. Use positive stops where possible. A *base setting* is the initial positioning of dies, stops, controls, guides, and so on. An *adjustment definition* is any change made to a base setting. To eliminate adjustments, make certain base settings are made exactly the same way each time a particular product is run.

9. Brainstorm and write down ideas to streamline internal and external time. Incorporate 5S techniques, visual controls, and POUS.

10. List ideas to test and adopt.

11. Results of setup time reduction based on improvement ideas. Look for improvements also in:

    - Ergonomics, safety

    - Poka-yoke

    - Positive stops

    - New location for tooling, jigs, paperwork, logs, checklists, and so on

    - Better staging

    - Color coding

    - Cycle-time reduction

    - Wear points and quick replacements

    - Process documentation of new (improved) setups to capture gains

    - Training requirements

    - First-piece inspection at machine

    - Jigs, fixtures, measuring devices, and so on

    - Ability of machine system to handle any part variations

12. Migrate to lean standard work.

Appendix B

5S Kaizen Event Workbook Example

This workbook is meant to be an example of forms, checklists, and worksheets that can be used during a 5S kaizen event. It is also a method to capture the results achieved by your team. By no means is it meant to be an all-inclusive workbook, but may be helpful for those pursuing 5S.

Workbook Cover

XYZ Company
Anytown, USA

5S Kaizen Event

5S in the Such-and-Such Department
Jan XX, 20XX–Jan XX,20XX

Project Leader
Eileen Improvement

Summary

Pre-Event Worksheet

Company	XYZ Company
Location/division	Anytown, USA
Event name	5S in the So-and-so Department
Event description	Organize and clean the so-and-so department
Target area	Such-and-such department supply storeroom
Date(s)	Jan XX, 20XX–Jan XX, 20XX

	Name	Department/position
Project leader	Eileen Improvement	
Lean champion		
Facilitator		
Team members		

Team photo

WEEK 1 MEETING AGENDA

- Team introductions
- Scope of project
  - Who, what, when, where, why, how?
  - Goals
  - Target area tour
  - Data collection requirements
- Brief overview of project
  - Overview method (presentation, video, books, articles)
- Expectations
- Communication methods
  - Communication with others not on the team
- Create or review pre-event checklist

WEEK 2

5S Supplies Checklist

Area/ ❏	Item	Quantity	Notes
Training room			
❏	LCD projector		
❏	Screen		
❏	Laptop		
❏	Flip chart		
❏	Markers		
❏	Large sticky notes		
❏	Medium size markers		
❏	Masking tape		
❏	Pens, pencils, and erasers		
❏	Clipboards		
❏	Rulers		
❏	Digital camera		
❏	Notepads		
❏	Lunch menu		
Sort			
❏	Red tags		
❏	Yellow, white, blue, manila tags		
❏	String, masking tape, wire to attach tags		
❏	Pens		
❏	Boxes to hold loose items		
❏	Red tag holding area sign		
❏	Masking tape or other		
Set-in-order			
❏	Yellow floor tape		
❏	Yellow/black floor tape		
❏	Red floor tape		
❏	White floor tape		
❏	Peel and stick letters		
❏	1" black or white letters		
❏	1" red letters		

Continued

Continued

Area/ ❑	Item	Quantity	Notes
❑	½" black or white letters		
❑	½" red letters		
❑	Line tape, black or red		
❑	Markers		
❑	Signs		
❑	Label maker		
❑	Backing board for signs		
❑	¼" plastic board for signs		
❑	Chain to hang sings		
❑	Magnetic boards		
❑	Peg board		
❑	Tools shadow stickers		
❑	Hooks		
❑	Tool holders		
❑	Dry erase board		
❑	Pouches to hold forms on board		
❑	Pipe labels		
❑	Hose reels		
❑	Safety signs		
❑	Direction arrows		
❑	Bins		
❑	Clear totes		
❑	Clear bins		
❑	Color coded filing system		
❑	Miscellaneous organizers		
❑	Miscellaneous tools		
❑	Job ticket holders (9" × 12")		
Shine			
❑	Cleaner, cleanser		
❑	Degreaser		
❑	Glass cleaner		
❑	Sprayers		
❑	Gloves		
❑	Masks		

Continued

Area/ ❏	Item	Quantity	Notes
❏	Scrubbing brushes		
❏	Scrapers		
❏	High-pressure sprayer, washer		
❏	Vacuum		
❏	Rags		
❏	Wipes, towels, paper towels		
❏	Sponges		
❏	Knee pads		
❏	Coveralls		
❏	Safety glasses		
❏	Ladders, lifts		
❏	Buckets		
❏	Brooms		
❏	Mops, warm water and soap		
❏	Floor cleaning machine		
❏	Floor squeegee		
❏	Trash cans		
❏	Shine cart/utility cart		
❏	5S supply cart		
Standardize			
❏	5S communication board		
❏	Floor paint		
❏	Paint rollers/brushes		
❏	Painter's tape		
Sustain			
❏	Reward and recognition items		
❏	5S books, videos, posters, pictures		
Outside resources			
❏	Electricians, mechanics, technicians		
❏	Riggers		
❏	Customer/suppliers/vendors		
❏	Other divisions, plants, locations		
❏	Consultants		
❏	Caterer		

Continued

Methods of communication	Leader
1. 5S communication board	
2. Short stand-up meetings with others from the area not on this team	
3. Memo to affected managers, supervisors and employees	
4. Announcement during companywide meeting	
5. Put article in newsletter	
6. Signs and posters: "Coming soon . . . improvement!"	
Metrics to track for improvement	**Leader**
1.	
2.	
3.	
4.	
5.	
6.	

Communication Poster

WEEK 3

- Review metrics
- Discuss obstacles to successful implementation
- Communicate with people in target area

ID	5S Vision
1	
2	
3	
4	
5	

WEEK 4—KAIZEN EVENT WEEK

Workplace Scan Assignments

Item	Assignment
Workplace information	
Spaghetti diagrams	
5S audit	
Photographs	
5S display board	

Spaghetti Diagram

Spaghetti diagram	
Product family	
Process	
Description	
Supplier	
Customer	
Drawn by:	
Date:	
Legend People Material Information	

Photograph Log

Before

After

Description

Description

Before

After

Description

Description

Before

After

Description

Description

Shine—Clean and Inspect Assignments

Task/Area	Team	Supplies needed

30-day action item list

Project:

Status
0 = Open	7
C = Closed	5
Total 12	
Complete 42%	

Classification	Count	Percent
A = No assistance needed	4	33.3%
B = Other resources needed	2	16.7%
C = Management help necessary	6	50.0%
Total	12	

Project Name

Classification legend:
☐ A = No assistance needed
☐ B = Other resources needed
☐ C = Management help necessary

Percent Complete — 32% / 68%

ID	Status	Classification	Priority	Description	Original completion date	Actual completion date	Percent	Assigned to (Primary)	Assigned to (Other)	Effort	Impact	Comments
				Organize								
10	C	A		Label the rack in pressroom				Graham	Pedro	L	H	
11	O	A		Have the plate maker separate bags by copy and color				Phil	John	L	H	
12	C	A		Different color sticky notes for each reason on hold				Graham	Pete, Maria P	L	H	Used colored clips
13	O	A		Mark and label cabinets				Roger	Pedro	L	L	Cabinets are new, need to decide what goes in
14	C	B		Have job bags pre-glued				John	Phil	L	L	Small only, can't glue medium or large
15	O	B		Organize area outside plate room				Phil	Homer	L	L	Cart parking area? Reduce WF damage in transit
16	O	C		Send e-mails when schedule is updated or changed				Roger	Robert	L	H	
17	O	C		Create final floor plan				John	Bob	M	M	
18	C	C		Move plate punches for better access				John	Steve	M	M	See #18
19	O	C		Install basket to catch proofs instead of falling on the floor				George	Ralph	L	L	
20	C	C		Figure out plate storage area with new processing line going in				Chris	Christy	M	M	See #18
21	O	C		Lock schedule after certain time (in the morning)				Roslyn	Lisa	H	H	

How to Sustain

ID	Idea
1	
2	
3	
4	
5	
6	
7	

Lessons Learned

ID	Lesson learned/opportunity for improvement	Comments/suggestions
	Sort	
1		
2		
3		
4		
5		
	Set in order	
1		
2		
3		
4		
5		
	Shine	
1		
2		
3		
4		
5		
	Standardize	
1		
2		
3		
4		
5		
	Sustain	
1		
2		
3		
4		
5		
	General	
1		
2		
3		
4		
5		

5S Results

Target area	So-and-so department.
Purpose	To help *estimate* the benefits achieved applying 5S workplace organization to the target area.
Directions	As a team, estimate the benefits achieved applying 5S to the target area from examples below (add more as necessary).

Benefit	Improvement (%, ↓, $, time, etc.)
5S resources	
5S standards	
Attitude	
Better cleanliness	
Better communication	
Better flow	
Better orderliness	
Better organization	
Better production flow	
Better quality	
Breakage, unusable, damage, obsolete items	
Color coding	
Ease of obtaining information/location	
Employee involvement	
Increased efficiency	
Increased safety	
Fewer breakdowns	
Less inventory	
Less search time	
Management support	
More ergonomic	
Pleasant place to work	
Point-of-use storage (POUS)	
Prevention of dirt, grime, and contamination	
Reward/recognition	
Sense of ownership	
Space saved	
Teamwork	
Useful inspections	
Visual controls	

Project Closeout

ID	Item	Rating				
1 = Very poor	2 = Poor 3 = Average 4 = Good 5 = Very good					
Vision		1	2	3	4	5
1	Did the end result meet the original desired results?					
2	Was the original plan realistic?					
3	How do others view the project?					
a	Customers					
b	Team members					
c	Stakeholders					
d	Other					
Plan		1	2	3	4	5
4	Project met budget specifications?					
5	Project met timeline specifications?					
6	Changes were successfully managed?					
7	Adequate resources were identified and utilized?					
Implementation		1	2	3	4	5
8	The plan was implemented successfully?					
9	The plan was revised sufficiently and in a timely manner?					
10	Resources were available?					
11	Review meetings were productive and regularly held?					
12	Project documentation was adequate?					
Close		1	2	3	4	5
13	The project ended in a timely manner?					
14	Project documentation was complete?					
15	All team members participated in project evaluation?					
16	Lessons learned and gaps were documented?					
17	Opportunities for improvements were documented and reviewed?					
Other		1	2	3	4	5

Comments:

Glossary

L ean is the foundation of a high-performance enterprise. In the simplest of terms, lean is the elimination of waste, and it is one of the best tools for improvement. The following glossary of terms will assist the reader in understanding lean concepts.

andon—A Japanese word meaning light or lantern. It is triggered by an abnormal condition or machine breakdown. It is a form of communication indicating that human intervention is required. Many times these are presented like a stoplight (red = stop, yellow = caution, green = go).

andon board—A visual control device in a production area, typically a lighted overhead display, indicating the current status of the production system and alerting team members to emerging problems, for example, takt awareness displays.

batch and queue—Producing more than one piece and then moving them to the next operation before they are needed there. Contrast with *single-piece flow.*

bottleneck—Any resource whose capacity is less than the demand placed on it.

cells—The layout of machines of different types for performing different operations in a tight sequence, typically in a U-shaped pattern. Cellular production permits single-piece flow, line balancing and flexible deployment of human effort by means of linked machines working efficiently based on takt time. Cell operators (who are cross-trained) may handle multiple processes, and the number of operators is changed when the customer demand rate changes.

change agent—The catalytic champion moving firms and value streams out of the world of batch and queue to flow manufacturing.

changeover—The term applies whenever a production device is assigned to perform a different operation or when the machine is set up to make a different part than the previous part. Examples would include: the installation of a new type of tool in a metalworking machine, a different paint in a painting system, a new plastic resin and a new mold in an injection-molding machine, new software in a computer, and so on.

changeover time—The time required to modify a system or workstation, usually including both teardown time for the existing condition and setup time for the new condition. It is measured from the run time of the last good piece of the current batch to the time of the first good piece of the next batch.

constraint—Anything that limits a system from achieving higher performance or throughput. Alternate definition: the bottleneck that most severely limits the organization's ability to achieve higher performance relative to its purpose/goal.

continuous flow production—A production system where products flow continuously rather than being separated into lots. No work in process is built up.

continuous improvement—A philosophy of making frequent and small changes to processes, the cumulative results of which lead to improved levels of quality, cost-effectiveness, and efficiency. Ongoing actions taken to find ways to improve processes, decrease variation, decrease cycle time, and improve effectiveness of the organization.

cycle—(1) A sequence of operations repeated regularly. (2) The time necessary for one sequence of operations to occur.

cycle time—The time required to complete one cycle of an operation. The time elapsing between a particular point in one cycle and the same point in the next cycle. If cycle time for every operation in a complete process can be reduced to equal *takt* time, products can be made in single-piece flow.

eight wastes—Taiichi Ohno's original enumeration of the seven wastes plus underutilized people. These are:

1. *Overproduction:* making more, earlier, or faster than the next operation needs it

2. *Waiting* for the next process, worker, material, information, or equipment

3. *Transportation*: unnecessary transport of materials

4. *Overprocessing* of anything that does not add value

5. *Inventories* more than the absolute minimum required to meet customer demand

6. *Motion*: unnecessary movement (like walking) of people

7. Production of *defective* parts or information

8. *Not fully utilizing employees'* brainpower, skills, experience, talents, and creativity

equipment availability—Machine operational availability is the percentage of time when a process (or equipment) is available to run. This is sometimes called *uptime*.

error detection—A hybrid form of error-proofing. It means that a bad part can be made, but it will be caught immediately and corrective action will be taken to avoid another bad part being produced. A device is put in place that detects when a bad part is made and then stops the process. This is used when error-proofing is too expensive or not easily implemented.

error-proofing—Helps to stabilize a process by preventing bad parts from being produced. With the use of error-proofing, operators can concentrate on production needs rather than being distracted by quality concerns. See also *poka-yoke*.

external setup—Setup procedures that can be performed while machine is running.

first-in, first-out (FIFO)—Means that material produced by one process is consumed in the same order by the next process. A FIFO queue is filled by the supplying process and emptied by the customer process. When a FIFO lane gets full, production is stopped until the next (internal) customer has used up some of that inventory.

first-pass yield (FPY)—Also referred to as the *quality rate,* is the percentage of units that complete a process and meet quality guidelines without being scrapped, rerun, retested, reworked, returned, or diverted into an off-line repair area. FPY is calculated by dividing the units entering the process minus the defective units by the total number of units entering the process.

5S—These are five Japanese words that begin with the letter S and translated to English as: *seiri* = sort, *seiton* = set in order, *seiso* = shine, *seiketsu* = standardize, *shitsuke* = sustain. Collectively they mean maintaining an orderly, well-inspected, clean, and efficient working environment.

heijunka—A method of leveling production for mix and volume.

hoshin kanri—The selection of goals, projects to achieve goals, designation of people and resources for project completion, and establishment of project metrics. Also called *policy deployment* in English.

information flow—The task of disseminating information for taking a specific product from order entry through scheduling to delivery. See *value stream.*

inspection—Comparing a product or component against specifications to determine if such a product or component meets requirements.

internal setup—Setup procedures that must be performed while a machine is stopped.

inventory—The money the firm has invested in purchasing things it intends to sell (raw materials, buffer stock, work in process, safety stock, and finished goods).

jidoka—This defect detection system automatically or manually stops production and/or equipment whenever an abnormal or defective condition arises. Any necessary improvements can then be made by directing attention to the stopped equipment and the worker who stopped the operation. The jidoka system posits faith in the worker as a thinker and allows all workers the right to stop the line on which they are working. It is now called *autonomation* in English.

just-in-time (JIT)—A philosophy that has the elimination of waste as its ultimate objective. To achieve this goal, each operation must be synchronized with those subsequent to it. The concept refers to the manufacturing and conveyance of only what is needed, when it is needed, and in the amount needed.

kaizen—Continuous, incremental improvement of an activity to create more value with less waste. A Japanese word or term meaning "change for the better." Many Japanese facilities view kaizen as the process of continually making incremental, ongoing changes and not as a single, separate event. Kaizen also strives to ensure quality and safety.

kaizen event—A short, focused, team-based improvement project that achieves breakthrough results. Also known as kaizen blitz, rapid kaizen, quick kaizen, and *kaikaku* in Japanese.

kanban—Kanban is a visual signal (for example, open space, two-bin, kanban cards) that ensures that every operation produces only the amount that will actually be used in the next step of the process. Kanban serves as indicator for both production and replenishment.

lead time—The time required for one piece to move all the way through a system of processes, from start to finish. The time from when the order is taken until the item is shipped.

lean—A systematic approach to identifying and eliminating waste (non-value-added activities) through continuous improvement in pursuit of perfection by flowing the product at the pull of the customer.

lean champion—Subject matter expert in the tools of lean typically chosen to lead lean training, lean projects, and lean transformation.

lean enterprise—Any organization that continually strives to eliminate waste, reduce costs, and improve quality, on-time delivery, and service levels.

lean production—The opposite of mass production.

level loading—A technique for balancing product mix and volume to capacity available.

line balancing—A process in which work elements are evenly distributed and staffing is balanced to meet takt time.

mass production—Large-scale manufacturing with high-volume production and output; implies traditional, even precomputer-era methods, with departmentalized operation and reliance on economies of scale to achieve low per-unit costs.

material requirements planning (MRP)—A computerized system typically used to determine the quantity and timing requirements for production and delivery of items (both customers and suppliers). Using MRP to schedule production at various processes will result in push production, since any predetermined schedule is only an estimate of what the next process will actually need.

manufacturing resource planning (MRP II)—MRP as just defined, plus capacity planning and a finance interface to translate operations planning into financial terms, and a simulation tool to assess alternate production plans. ERP is enterprisewide resource planning, going beyond the shop floor.

muda—A Japanese word, usually translated as "waste," that refers to those elements of production that do not add value to the product.

non-value-added—Activities or actions taken that add no real value to the product or service, making such activities or actions a form of waste. See *value-added*.

overall equipment effectiveness (OEE)—A machine's overall equipment effectiveness is the product of its operational availability, performance efficiency, and first-pass yield. See *total productive maintenance*.

point-of-use storage (POUS)—Having information, items, materials, parts, and tools stored near where they are used.

poka-yoke (error-proofing)—Low-cost, highly reliable devices or innovations that can either detect abnormal situations before they occur in a production process, or, if they occur, will stop the machines or equipment and prevent the production of defective products, those that prevent errors by an operator, and those that detect errors by an operator and give a warning, and those that detect defects in products and prevent further processing of them.

production (analysis) board—This is a board located at a job site on which hourly production targets are recorded along with the actual production achieved. It is a good example of visual management. Also known as a 60-minute board.

productivity—A measurement of output for a given amount of input(s). Increases in productivity are considered critical to raising living standards.

pull—A system of cascading production and delivery instructions from downstream to upstream activities in which the upstream supplier does not produce until the downstream customer signals a need. The opposite of push.

quick changeover—The ability to change dies, tooling, and fixtures rapidly (usually in minutes), so smaller batch sizes can be produced effectively.

right size—Matching tooling, people, and equipment to the job and space requirements of lean production. It does *not* mean downsize.

runner—A person on the production floor who paces the entire value stream, from the pickup and delivery of materials through kanban utilization. Also known as a *material handler* or *water spider.*

shadow board—A board painted to indicate which tool belongs where and which tools are missing. A visual management tool.

single minute exchange of dies (SMED)—A series of techniques pioneered by Shigeo Shingo for changeovers of production machinery in less than 10 minutes. The long-term objective is always zero setup, in which changeovers are instantaneous and do not interfere in any way with continuous flow. SMED means changing dies in single digits, meaning nine minutes or less, rather than a single minute.

single-piece flow—A situation in a lean enterprise where products proceed one complete unit at a time through various operations in design, order taking, and production, without interruptions, backflows, or scrap. In lean manufacturing, this is the antithesis of batch-and-queue production.

spaghetti diagram—A drawing commonly used to uncover motion and transportation wastes that shows the layout and flow of material, information, and people in a work area.

standard work—A precise description of each work activity, specifying cycle time, takt time, the work sequence of specific tasks, and the minimum inventory of parts on hand needed to conduct the activity. All jobs are organized around human motion to create an efficient sequence without waste.

standardization—When policies and common procedures are used to manage processes throughout the system.

supermarkets—The storage locations of parts before they go on to the next operation. They are managed by predetermined maximum and minimum (or order point and order quantity) inventory levels.

takt time—The available production time divided by the rate of customer demand. Takt time sets the pace of production to match the rate of customer demand and becomes the heartbeat of any lean system.

theory of constraints—A management philosophy that stresses removal of constraints to increase throughput while decreasing inventory and operating expenses.

throughput—The rate the system generates money through sales (or the conversion rate of inventory into shipped product).

total productive maintenance (TPM)—A system to ensure that every machine in a production process is always able to perform its required tasks so that production is never interrupted. Uptime is maximized, along with machine performance and first-pass yield. See *overall equipment effectiveness.*

value—A capability provided to a customer at the right time at an appropriate price, as defined in each case by the customer.

value stream—The set of specific actions required to bring a specific product from raw material to finished goods per customer demand, concentrating on information management and physical transformation tasks.

value stream map (VSM)—A drawing using icons that shows the information flow and material flow of a process family (similar processing steps) in an organization.

value-added—Activities or actions taken that add real value to the product or service. See *non-value-added.*

visual control/management—The placement in plain view of all tools, parts, production activities, and indicators of production system performance, so everyone involved can understand the status of the system at a glance. This is a concept whereby managers can tell immediately if production activities are proceeding normally or not. Lines, signs and labels, andon, kanban, production boards, painted floors, and shadow boards are typical visual control tools.

waste—Any activity that consumes resources, but creates no value. Any activity that utilizes equipment, materials, parts, space, employee time, or other corporate resource beyond the minimum amount required for value-added operations and for which the customer is unwilling to pay.

Bibliography

Conner, Gary. *Lean Manufacturing for the Small Shop.* Dearborn, MI: Society of Manufacturing Engineers, 2001.

Dennis, Pascal. *Lean Production Simplified: A Plain-Language Guide to the World's Most Powerful Production System.* New York: Productivity Press, 2002.

Imai, Masaaki. *Gemba Kaizen: A Commonsense, Low-Cost Approach to Management.* New York: McGraw-Hill, 1997.

———. *Kaizen: The Key to Japan's Competitive Success.* New York: McGraw-Hill/Irwin, 1986.

Liker, Jeffrey K. *Becoming Lean: Inside Stories of U.S. Manufacturers.* Portland, OR: Productivity Inc., 1998.

———. *The Toyota Way: 14 Management Principles from The World's Greatest Manufacturer.* New York: McGraw-Hill, 2004.

Ohno, Taiichi. *Toyota Production System: Beyond Large-Scale Production.* New York: Productivity Press, 1988.

Rother, Mike, and John Shook. *Learning to See Version 1.3.* Brookline, MA: Lean Enterprise Institute, 2003.

Womack, James P., and Daniel T. Jones. *Lean Thinking: Banish Waste and Create Wealth in Your Corporation.* New York: Simon & Schuster, 1996.

Womack, James P., Daniel T. Jones, and Daniel Roos. *The Machine That Changed the World: The Story of Lean Production.* New York: HarperCollins 1990.

Index

A

accounting credits, kaizen event
    example, 53–59
agenda, kaizen event example, 89–90
arrow analysis, 129

B

batch-size reduction, 7
    exercise, 63–65
benefits, kaizen event, examples, 52,
    58–59
brainstorming
    definition, 17
    for future state, in kaizen event, 37
    kaizen event examples, 84, 90
    methods, 17–19
brainstorming techniques, in kaizen
    events, 17–20
breakthrough improvement
    (kaizen), versus continuous
    improvement, 10
building blocks of lean, 6–8

C

cellular design
    definition, 7
    five-step process, 65–69
    kaizen event example, 59–70
change management, and kaizen
    teams, 13–16

changeover time, definition, 5
communication, in kaizen event, 34,
    41–42
consensus, definition, 19
continuous improvement, versus
    kaizen (breakthrough
    improvement), 10
cost–benefit analysis, of kaizen
    events, 125–29
creativity before capital, 9, 17
current state, assessment
    in kaizen event, 36–37
    kaizen event examples, 61–62,
        71–75, 78–79, 82–84, 88–89,
        91–94, 99–100, 107–8
customer service, standard work in,
    kaizen event example, 91–98

D

delivery, kaizen event example, 88–91

E

effort and impact matrix, 37, 38
eight deadly wastes, 3–4

F

five whys, example, 23
5M, visual management in, examples,
    123–24

5S workplace organization and standardization
  benefits worksheet, 128–29
  definition, 7
  kaizen event example, 46–52
  kaizen event workbook example, 145–58
future state
  brainstorming for, in kaizen event, 37
  kaizen event example, 108

G

goals, kaizen event examples, 72–73, 78, 91, 102–3

J

just-in-time (JIT) manufacturing, in Toyota Production System, 21

K

kaizen, definition, 10
  versus continuous improvement, 10
kaizen blitz. *See* kaizen event
kaizen event
  brainstorming for future state, 37
  brainstorming techniques in, 17–20
  closeout and presentation, 38–40, 42–44
  communication in, 34, 41–42
  cost–benefit analysis of, 125–29
  current state, assessment, 36–37
  definition, 11
  eight-week cycle, 28
  follow-up, 40–41
  how to perform, 27–44
  implementation, 37–38
  lean champion, 29
  materials needed, 32–34
  metrics, 34–35

  pre-event preparation, 28–29
  project definition, 31–32
  project leader, 29
  reward and recognition, 42–44
  team members, 29–30
  team rules for, 19
  training, 36, 41–42
  week 1, 31–32
  week 2, 32–35
  week 3, 35
  week 4, 35–40
    schedule, 35–36
  weeks 5, 6, and 7, 40–42
  week 8, 42–44
kaizen event examples, 45–124
  accounting credits, 53–59
  cellular design, 59–70
  5S workbook, 145–58
  5S workplace organization and standardization, 46–52
  layout, 70–76
  quick changeover, 80–88
  quick changeover workbook, 133–43
  request for quote to order entry, 76–80
  shipping, delivery, and logistics, 88–91
  standard work in customer service, 91–98
  total productive maintenance, 99–106
  value stream mapping, RFQ to delivery, 106–9
kaizen teams, 15–16, 29–30
  charter, 32
  versus daily work teams, 15
  definition, 15
  reward and recognition of, 42–44
kanban (pull) system, definition, 7

L

layout, kaizen event example, 70–76
lead time, reducing non-value-added, 10

lean
benefits of, 1–2
building blocks of, 6–8
combining with other
improvement efforts,
xiv, 6
core concepts, xv, 9–10
definition, 1–2
history, xiii, 2
importance of, in today's economy,
2–3
origins, xiii
wastes of, 3–6
lean baseline assessment, 8–9
lean champion, in kaizen event, 29
lean enterprise, 10
definition, 2
lean implementation
factors for successful, xiv,
14–15
how to start, 8–9
role of change management in,
13–15
lean journey. *See* lean
implementation
lean kaizen, in Toyota Production
System, 21–25
lean transformation. *See* lean
implementation
lessons learned, kaizen event
examples, 70, 88, 97, 104–6
line balancing, kaizen event example,
66–68
logistics, kaizen event example,
88–91

M

materials, needed for kaizen event,
32–34
metrics, in kaizen event, 34–35
muda, 3–4

O

"one good idea" sheet, 103–4

one-page summary, 49
one-point lesson, 41–42
example, 50
overprocessing waste, example, 48

P

point-of-use storage (POUS),
definition, 7
problem solving, emphasis in
Toyota Production System,
21–22
project closeout, in kaizen event,
42–44
project definition, in kaizen event,
31–32
project leader, in kaizen event, 29
pull (kanban) system, definition, 7

Q

quality at the source, definition, 7
quality tools
use of in kaizen event, 20
use of in Toyota Production
System, 22–25
quick changeover (QCO)
definition, 7
improvement process, 5–6
kaizen event example, 80–88
workbook example, 133–43
quick kaizen. *See* kaizen event

R

request for quote to order entry,
kaizen event example,
76–80
resistance to standard work, reasons
for, 96
results, kaizen event, examples,
69–70, 76, 86–87, 90–91,
94–97, 108–9
reward and recognition, of kaizen
team members, 42–44

S

seven (eight) deadly wastes, 3–4
shipping, kaizen event example,
88–91
single-minute exchange of dies
(SMED) technique, 5
cost–benefit example, 126–27
quick changeover workbook
example, 133–43
spaghetti diagram, 24
standard work
in customer service, kaizen event
example, 91–98
definition, 7
resistance to, reasons for, 96
streamlined layout, definition, 7

T

takt time, kaizen event example, 66
team
members, in kaizen event,
29–30
rules for kaizen event, 19
team charter, in kaizen event, 32
total productive maintenance (TPM)
definition, 8
kaizen event example, 99–106
Toyota Motor Company, 2

Toyota Production System (TPS)
lean kaizen in, 21–25
origin, xiii, 2
training, in kaizen event, 36, 41–42

V

value stream map (VSM), 8
value stream mapping
four-step process, 107
kaizen event example, 106–9
variation, waste due to, 6
visual controls
definition, 7
examples, 113–20
exercise, 110–13
kaizen event example, 109–24
visual workplace
checklist, 120–24
kaizen event example, 109–24

W

walk-through, benefit to kaizen event,
53–54
waste, due to variation, 6
wastes of lean, 3–6
kaizen event examples, 71–72
seven (eight) deadly wastes, 3–4